The North Korea Crisis and Regional Responses

EDITED BY

Utpal Vyas
Ching-Chang Chen
Denny Roy

EAST-WEST CENTER
COLLABORATION · EXPERTISE · LEADERSHIP

The North Korea Crisis and Regional Responses
Utpal Vyas, Ching-Chang Chen, and Denny Roy, editors

ISBN 978-0-86638-254-0 (print) and 978-0-86638-255-7 (electronic)

The views expressed in this volume are those of the authors and not necessarily those of the sponsors or the publisher.

Free electronic files of the volume are available on the East-West Center website: EastWestCenter.org/Publications

Publications Office
East-West Center
1601 East-West Road
Honolulu, Hawai'i 96848-1601
Tel: 808.944.7145
EWCBooks@EastWestCenter.org

EastWestCenter.org

The **East-West Center** promotes better relations and understanding among the people and nations of the United States, Asia, and the Pacific through cooperative study, research, and dialogue. Established by the US Congress in 1960, the Center serves as a resource for information and analysis on critical issues of common concern, bringing people together to exchange views, build expertise, and develop policy options.

The Center's 21-acre Honolulu campus, adjacent to the University of Hawai'i at Mānoa, is located midway between Asia and the US mainland and features research, residential, and international conference facilities. The Center's Washington, DC, office focuses on preparing the United States for an era of growing Asia Pacific prominence.

Contents

Preface / 1

1   Sources and Objectives of North Korea Foreign Policy: Identity,
     Values, and Negotiating Behavior / 3
     Jina KIM

2   North Korea's Nuclear Development, the Non-Proliferation Treaty
     Regime, and Regional Security / 20
     Shinichi OGAWA

3   Humanitarian Implications of the North Korea Problem / 37
     Utpal VYAS

4   Strategic Ramifications of the North Korea Nuclear Weapons
     Crisis / 53
     Denny ROY

5   Economic Engagement with North Korea / 70
     Yoshinori KASEDA

6   The North Korea Problem from South Korea's Perspective / 88
     Jihwan HWANG

7   The North Korea Problem and China: Interests, Debates, and
     Roadmaps / 100
     ZHENG Jiyong

8   Explaining Japan's North Korea Policy / 114
     Yoichiro SATO

9   North Korea's Nuclear Weapons and the United States: More
     Difficult, More Complicated, and More Dangerous / 130
     Nicholas HAMISEVICZ

10   Unwitting Bedfellows: Taiwan and the North Korea Problem / 145
     Ching-Chang CHEN

11   Common Interest Without Coordination / 160
     Utpal VYAS, Ching-Chang CHEN, and Denny ROY

     List of Contributors / 165

Acronyms

ADB	Asian Development Bank
AIT	American Institute in Taiwan
ASEAN	Association of Southeast Asian Nations
CCP	Chinese Communist Party
CMC	Central Military Commission
DPRK	Democratic People's Republic of Korea (North Korea)
FTA	Free Trade Area
GDP	gross domestic product
IAEA	International Atomic Energy Agency
ICBM	intercontinental ballistic missile
ICC	International Criminal Court
ICISS	International Commission on Intervention and State Sovereignty
KIC	Kaesong Industrial Complex
KIS	Kim Il Sung
KJI	Kim Jong Il
KJU	Kim Jong Un
KMT	Kuomintang (Chinese Nationalist Party)
KOTRA	Korea Trade-Investment Promotion Agency
KPA	Korean People's Army (DPRK)
KWP	Korea Workers' Party (ruling party of the DPRK)
LDP	Liberal Democratic Party of Japan
MNA	multilateral nuclear approach
NDC	National Defense Commission (DPRK)
NGO	nongovernmental organization
NLL	Northern Limit Line
NNWS	non-nuclear weapons state

NPT	Non-Proliferation Treaty on Nuclear Weapons
NWS	nuclear weapons state
PLA	People's Liberation Army
PRC	People's Republic of China
R2P	responsibility to protect
ROC	Republic of China
ROK	Republic of Korea
SEZ	special economic zone
6PT	Six-Party Talks
TCOG	Trilateral Coordination and Oversight Group
TMD	Theater Missile Defense
UNDP	United Nations Development Program
UNFAO	United Nations Food and Agriculture Organization
UNHRC	United Nations Human Rights Council
UNICEF	United Nations Children's Fund
UNSC	United Nations Security Council
WFP	UN World Food Program
USFK	United States Forces Korea
WMD	weapons of mass destruction

Preface

The governments of Northeast Asia agree that North Korea's development of nuclear weapons and missiles to carry them makes the region more dangerous. Bringing about the denuclearization of the Democratic People's Republic of Korea (DPRK) is therefore a common interest of governments in the region. International cooperation on strategic issues is notoriously difficult to achieve, especially in a region that lacks a mature multilateral security organization. Similarly, although the humanitarian crisis in the DPRK caused by massive human rights violations and economic mismanagement evokes sympathy for the North Korean people, the costs and politics of multilateral intervention remain insuperable.

Nevertheless, the North Korea case would seem to offer an unusually favorable chance of success in rallying Asia-Pacific governments to pull together, because the levels of both urgency and unanimity are high. The prospects of success in such an effort are determined by the interests of these individual governments. Even if they agree on the general preferred outcome, each has its own reasons for supporting or opposing particular strategies and tactics.

Accordingly, this monograph considers the viewpoints of various governments while examining the broader question of whether an effective regional response to the DPRK crisis is possible. The principal finding is that the conflicting national interests that have precluded a successful coordinated multilateral policy thus far will continue to leave Pyongyang in dangerous, angry isolation even after it attains a credible nuclear intercontinental ballistic missile capability.

This volume is the result of a project that began as an international workshop in 2013 hosted by Ritsumeikan Asia Pacific University (APU) in Beppu, Japan. The co-editors are grateful to APU and to the East-West Center for co-sponsoring this workshop. Publication of the volume was made possible by an APU Academic Publication Subsidy and the East-West Center Publications Office. The co-editors also would like to thank APU student Nina C. Krickel for her valuable editorial assistance.

CHAPTER I

Sources and Objectives of North Korea Foreign Policy

Identity, Values, and Negotiating Behavior

Jina KIM

The Kim Jong Un (KJU) regime, since its inception, has ratcheted up tension on the Korean Peninsula. His decision to dishonor what he had agreed to—a moratorium on nuclear tests and long-range missile launches as well as the return of IAEA (International Atomic Energy Agency) inspectors to Yongbyon—at several rounds of bilateral talks with the United States in February 2012 confirmed the belief that North Korea is a historically unpredictable and unreliable actor. Because the new North Korean leadership needed to fulfill its promise that North Korea would enter an "era of being a strong and prosperous nation (*gangseongdaeguk*)," pursuing economic recovery by easing tension through reconciliation with the international community, including the United States, was of significance. North Korea could have obtained nutritional assistance including corn, soy beans, vegetable oils, and ready-to-eat therapeutic food, but instead it initiated a string of provocations and hostile threats, which brought China's patience to the limits, strengthened UN sanctions, and consolidated the US position not to engage with North Korea before Pyongyang shows concrete steps for denuclearization. Hence, for the international observers, North Korea's gamble seemed to be a grave mistake.

Arguably, the sudden death of Kim Jong Il (KJI) and the accession to power of KJU made North Korea even more unpredictable. Because the international media expected that the Western-educated North Korean leader would move the country toward more reform and openness, North Korea's attempt to amplify its rhetorical threats against South Korea and the United States increased the uncertainty regarding North Korea's future course of actions. Indeed, foreign policy analysts seem to split on whether the last wave of threats from December 2012 to April 2013, including nullifying the armistice treaty and cutting hot-lines between the two Koreas is indicative of North Korea's intention to escalate tension toward a possible military confrontation, or a much-calculated diplomatic maneuver. Besides, North Korea's recent charm offensive confuses those who believed that KJU would not take his country in a new direction. Hence, in response to North Korea's proposal to hold talks for cross-border family reunions and halting all acts of slander against each other, the South Korea media was skeptical because North Korea also demanded South Korea unilaterally call off South Korea–US military exercises, which has been part of a cycle—peaceful gesture followed by provocation. Therefore, examining whether North Korea is genuine about peaceful rapprochement and analyzing sources and objectives of North Korea's foreign policy with theoretical and historical approaches is more important than ever.

PUZZLES AND CONSTRUCTIVIST APPROACH

Taking a closer look into the history of North Korea's foreign relations, one can note that it is full of contradiction and complexity. North Korea deepened its self-imposed isolation, but it also heavily relied on foreign aid and assistance. It first joined the NPT (Non-Proliferation Treaty on Nuclear Weapons) and then withdrew from it; it agreed on denuclearization and then abandoned opportunities for improving its relations with others; it developed nuclear weapons at the risk of provoking its regional neighbors and alienated further the international community despite the urgent need for international aid. Nonetheless, to a certain degree, North Korea has demonstrated a consistent behavioral pattern despite changes and shifts in its surrounding conditions. Hence, first of all, this chapter will explain various approaches to understand the way that North Korea conducts its relations with other states, and will show that North Korea's foreign policy behavior can be examined with a constructivist approach.

Interest-Based Prism

The prism through which the international community viewed North Korea was mostly nuclear brinkmanship diplomacy. However, whether North Korea's behavior is driven by the structural context as it contends or Pyongyang is just playing a game of so-called brinkmanship needs thorough examination. Realist approaches explain a state's response to an existential threat as an effort to secure useful shields against adversarial aggression, or to balance against a powerful rival. As Rosecrance notes, North Korea, with a long history of engaging in military confrontation, may be actively seeking nuclear weapons as a means of terminating a struggle with its foe[1] or, as Goheen observes, it may be passively compelled to develop a similar capability of its own to protect itself from its adversary's military threat.[2] However, North Korea's behavior, so incomprehensible that one cannot decipher it, cannot be construed simply as a reaction to the external stimulus. Epstein writes that non-nuclear countries without a nuclear umbrella feel that they may ultimately have to rely on nuclear weapons.[3] According to this logic, North Korea would become one of the nuclear candidates that are concerned foremost with their unique security concerns.[4] However, such views do not adequately explain why North Korea's nuclear crisis broke out when tension on the Korean Peninsula began to thaw or why North Korea pursued nuclear and missile capabilities at the risk of embarrassing China and Russia. In this regard, to interest-based theorists, Pyongyang's seemingly confusing decision seems like an anomaly.

Neoliberal institutionalism's utilitarian approaches can also provide a partial explanation of North Korea's strategic mind. It is in North Korea's interest to participate in the Six-Party Talks because it could reap gains by cooperating with the others.[5] However, the rationale focusing on cost-benefit calculation of the states does not adequately explain why North Korea stepped back from the 1994 Geneva Agreed Framework and from the 9.19 Agreement through the Six-Party Talks in 2005 despite promised rewards. North Korea's defiance of nonproliferation efforts of the international community counters the belief that small states may view themselves as the beneficiaries of a collective good offered by institutions, believing that it gives them legitimacy and power.[6] Indeed, the framework based on the assumption of states' rationality does not take into account how principles and norms are actually perceived by North Korea.

Constructivist Prism

North Korea's preferences, interests, and identities are taken as stable within a rational framework, but social constructivism suggests that states with difficulties forming positive identification may not construct the same kinds of perceptions and attitudes. States, by positively identifying themselves with others, confirm their positional status as respected group member states. However, social identities can be either cooperative or conflictual, and identification is a continuum from negative to positive.[7] The logical progression of this train of thought suggests that antipathy and distrust lead a state to sustain a competitive identity and show noncompliant behavior. North Korea's unique identity and values allow it to diverge from international principles and standards. North Korea identifies its interests negatively with regard to those of the others, and hence North Korea's flaunting of international demands can be examined in this light.

OBJECTIVES OF NORTH KOREA'S FOREIGN POLICY

In an antagonistic structure where legitimacy competition goes on between the two Koreas, three of its primary goals maintain North Korea's continuing status as a revisionist state: (1) to seek ways to compensate for its inferiority in conventional forces with the development of asymmetric capability; (2) to drive a wedge between Seoul and Washington to weaken domestic support for the US military presence in the South; (3) to utilize opportunities to infuse revolutionary ideas and cause disunity (so-called South-South conflict) within South Korean society.

Duality of National Interests

Revisionist goals. Since the Korean War, North Korea has pursued a revisionist path—the establishment of a unified state by force. Although North Korea turned into a status-quo oriented power during postwar rehabilitation and revitalization of its economy, North Korea resumed its revisionist tendencies and during these periods there were signs of political instability in the North. When North Korea was undergoing power transition, having problems with economic management, and tightening control of its people to forestall social instability, aggressiveness in its foreign policy was also noticeable, for example when Kim Il Sung (KIS) struggled to build a monolithic leadership among a number of factions that vied for total control of state power, and when KJI became the leader of a nation that was hit hard by an economic breakdown and mass starvation in the 1990s when widespread famine killed more than 10 percent of the population. The December 2012–April 2013 crisis on the Korean Peninsula coincided with KJU's legitimacy-building campaign to tighten his grip on his cohorts.

North Korea's aggressiveness can also be examined in light of its ceaseless attempts to delegitimize the South. The fact that the two Koreas engage in legitimacy competition makes North Korea perceive South Korea's goal of absorption of the other half of the Peninsula as an existential threat. The two Koreas claim to be the sole legitimate governments for the entire Korean Peninsula, and North Korea's foremost concern has been resolving the Korea division in its favor. Indeed, North Korea has employed a variety of covert and overt operations against the South since political instability in the South emerged in the 1960s and 1970s.[8] In the recent rhetoric from North Korea its goal of revolutionizing the South is rarely mentioned, and North Korea's communist influence on the South remains negligible. However, Pyongyang has not officially abandoned its goal to instill revolutionary spirit throughout the Korean Peninsula. North Korea's socialist constitution states that Kim Il Sung is the founder of socialist Korea and the entire Korean people will defend and carry forward his idea and complete the Juche (self-reliance) revolution.[9] Small-scale but lethal attacks against South Korea have been a feature of North Korea's approach since the 1960s.

Pragmatic goals. North Korea utilized diplomatic outreach as part of efforts to achieve pragmatic goals—diplomatic recognition and foreign aid. North Korea's Socialist Constitution stipulates, "Independence, peace and solidarity are the basic ideals of the foreign policy and the principles of external activities of the DPRK."[10] It was at the first session of the 9th Supreme People's Assembly in 1990 when North Korea changed the order from "solidarity and peace," and this change indicates a change in North Korea's strategic calculus, to develop working relationships with non-communist states. Being a resourceful supplier of military equipment and expertise to resistance movements in the Third World, North Korea used military assistance programs as an instrument of foreign policy in the 1960s and 1970s.[11] Expanding diplomatic relations served the purpose of taking the upper hand over South Korea in terms of legitimacy competition.

It should be noted that North Korea's diplomatic outreach since the 1980s was employed to attract foreign investment by establishing full diplomatic relations with capitalist states. In the period of regime change in East Europe, North Korea aimed to remove threats on the Korean Peninsula and create a favorable environment for the restoration of its economy by normalizing relations with the United States and Japan. KIS enacted the Law of Equity Joint Venture and Foreign Investment Bank Act in 1984 and the Law on Foreign Investment in October 1992 in order to induce the investment of capital by foreign governments and corporations. KJI also made similar attempts including revision of laws and regulations, reshuffling of the administration system in the mid-2000s, and institutionalization for development and management of the Rajin-Sunbong Special Economic Zone in 2010. In a similar fashion, KJU has tried to attract foreign investment by constructing ski and beach resorts and setting up fourteen special economic zones across the country. Diplomatic breakthrough could open a gate for improving economic conditions, reducing the threat alert level, and concentrating resources on other key areas. Hence, North Korea alternately chose its actions for both revolutionary and practical goals. Consequently, North Korea's foreign relations have gone through a dialectical course, shifting between negative and positive interactions.

Continuity and Changes

What frustrated the international community was North Korea's vacillating attitude between revisionist and pragmatic approaches, such as setting off a naval skirmish following an inter-Korea Red Cross meeting in October 2009 and shelling Yeonpyeong Island after the reunion of separated families in October 2010. However, it should also be noted that these are not isolated events and North Korea's unique situation prompts it to consider multiple goals: (1) making a breakthrough in diplomatic and economic relations, (2) seeking a turning point to regain international attention, and at the same time (3) fending off external influence caused by partial openness. In the end, these two approaches are not distinct but related in light of the embodiment of North Korea's ruling ideology Juche[12] through reinterpretation and adaptation. For Pyongyang watchers, North Korea's foreign policy is full of abnormality. To understand North Korea's erratic behavior, one needs to look at the uniqueness of North Korea's foreign policy decision-making process.

Leader-dominant (*yuil cheje*) system. It is hard to imagine that North Korea's foreign policy is a product of debates among those in charge of various state responsibilities. In North Korea, the leader exercises supreme authority in every domain, and foreign policy decision is not an exception. North Korea's Supreme People's Assembly has the legal authority to establish the basic principles of foreign policies, ratify treaties, and appoint as well as recall ambassadors to foreign states,[13] and the cabinet conducts general guidance in the sphere of relations with foreign states.[14] However, it is the KWP (Korea Worker's Party) Central Committee's politburo that approves North Korea's foreign policy, and the supreme leader who presides over the politburo holds the ultimate power of policymaking responsibility. This is a protocol that needs to be sustained in order not to endanger his position and keep the stability of the regime.

Like his predecessors, KJU solidified his control over the North Korean elites through purges and the appointment of loyal supporters. This means that there is little room for multiple competing views to be presented in the decision-making process. His position of First Secretary of the KWP,

Chairman of the Central Military Commission (CMC), and First Chairman of the National Defense Commission (NDC) gives him the power to rule without obvious challenges. CMC and NDC decision making is done at the same time to ensure that the military follows the Party's lead, which means that both institutions serve in a coordination and facilitation role that ensures the enforcement of orders made higher up the chain of command—i.e., by the supreme leader of North Korea. Hence, competition among political parties, private groups, and bureaucrats is not very useful for the study of North Korea.

One may argue that personal judgment is also bounded by specific context of the surrounding environment.[15] This implies that the antagonistic structure in which North Korea lies produces the repetitive pattern of temporal compromise and setbacks from agreed measures. KJU's speech on 15 April 2012, which stressed that the North Korean people would no longer have to tighten their belts, was understood as an expression of his willingness not to push the limits regarding the international community. However, KJU's decision to go further than his father by unconditionally abrogating the Armistice Treaty indicates that the new supreme leader can hardly move away from the patterns of the past. It can be argued that North Korea's foreign policy decision making is affected by what the supreme leader values most – dealing with the challenge to the throne, finding legitimacy as a protector of North Korea's political ideology, ensuring continuity of the long-held communist system, and so on.

Path dependency. It has been only three years since KJU came to power, but analyzing and predicting the new leadership's foreign policy is possible given the consistency of the structural conditions and ideational factors that affect North Korea's policy decision-making process. One may be confused by the reports that North Korea strengthens leadership of the party over the military as an indication of change from a "military-first" to a "party-first" stance.[16] A reference to military-first (Songun) politics was added to the party charter, which now says that "the Party will establish military-first politics as a basic political system of socialism."[17] On the anniversary of the military-first doctrine, KJU stressed again that the leadership of the KWP is essential for the Korean People's Army (KPA) and that the two are inseparable. However, these changes should not be interpreted as a sign of shifting balance of power because there has never been a case where the party's supremacy was overtaken by the military in North Korea's history. Where the supreme leader directs his order changes, but what he orders may not. It should be noted that empowerment of the NDC was designed to give KJI, Chairman of the NDC, more power to rule. Since his designation as an heir apparent, KJU began his leadership career as a head of the KWP's CMC, which became a critical institution wherefrom he consolidated and exercised his power. North Korea's foreign policy decision making is performed by a purposeful agent who acts with certain policy concepts.

SOURCES OF NORTH KOREA'S FOREIGN POLICY: STRUCTURAL CO-CONSTITUTION AND INTERACTIVE PATTERNS

Negative Identification and Antagonistic Structure

North Korea's attitude toward the outside depends not only on the cognitive prism through which it understands the significance of compliance to external demands but also on its position in relation to the other members of the international community. Positive identification occurs "when an individual accepts influence because he wants to establish or to maintain a satisfying self-defining relationship to another person or group."[18] However, North Korea has long experienced difficulties in forming a collective social identity through positive interactions with other states. Hence, having a "corporate identity,"[19] North Korea held pre-existing ideas about its national identity that guided its behavior toward the others, and the negative interactions that it experienced consolidated its negative identity.[20]

First, the unique circumstance of North Korea as a highly militarized but small, weak country with a history of territorial invasion surrounded by super powers created North Korea's unique identity.[21] A state of alienation from its patrons and competition with South Korea worsened after the Cold War when North Korea's leadership assumed responsibility to lead the country without dependence on external input. The lasting Cold War legacy on the Korean Peninsula made it impossible for North Korea to negotiate with the West on friendly terms, and the intricate relationship between the two Koreas involves the North-South rivalry and an absence of a trust-building mechanism.[22]

Second, reliance on the past hinders North Korea from making a complete departure from the past. KJI justified his power based on the legacy of KIS and consistently claimed his father's mantle to legitimize the dynastic transition.[23] Particularly after the second nuclear crisis broke out, KJI perpetuated his identification with his father through extensive propaganda. KJU, like his father, relied heavily on KIS's legacy. For the first two years, he tried to mimic his grandfather's gestures and appearance to invoke North Korea's nostalgia for the relatively well-off era in the past. Emphasis on Songun during the KJI era continued for the first two years of the KJU regime.

Third, identifying North Korea as a tyrant regime brought huge repercussions. North Korea often mentioned that President Bush's "part of an axis of evil" rhetoric and Secretary Condoleezza Rice's reference to North Korea as one of the world's "outposts of tyranny" were little short of declarations of war.[24] Branding North Korea as a "rogue" could mean "denial of recognition" of the North Korean regime as a negotiating partner, and Pyongyang warned that it would not engage in a dialogue unless the United States showed it due respect.[25] Although the Obama administration does not openly make verbal attacks on North Korea, the freedom agenda endorsed by those who had significant influence on US policy continues to antagonize North Korea, worsening its negative identification. The policy to spread democracy in countries under authoritarian regimes was viewed by North Korea as a grave threat to the regime and feared as an act of interference and a threat of contamination.[26]

In addition, a complicated triangular relationship among the United States and two Koreas shaped an antagonistic structure in which check and balance, rather than cooperation based on shared interests, is dominant. On the one hand, North Korea is obsessed with fears of a concerted US-South Korea effort to promote its collapse.[27] On the other hand, North Korea sees normalization of diplomatic relations with the United States as a critical component of keeping stability of its system. South Korea was in a position to consolidate its military alliance with the United States as the tension on the Korean Peninsula increased, but Seoul's reaching out to Washington, not to Pyongyang, was viewed as an "act of betrayal" by North Korea.[28]

Rally-Around-the-Flag Effect and Trade-Off in Decision Making

It is more likely that when the regime is weak politically and tries to avoid blame for its mismanagement, it will seek ways to consolidate support by means of the rally-around effect. Confrontation with external foes helps North Korea reconfirm internal unity.[29] North Korea's nationalist response indicates that its leadership uses external threats to strengthen domestic support from the populace, places the blame for economic instability on the outsider, and directs resentment toward those who have imposed the sanctions.[30] The first nuclear crisis broke out when Pyongyang was newly vulnerable, and North Korea held rallies among secretaries of party cells, for the first time since the founding day of the KWP in June 1949, in order to stress "their duties to give loyalty to the party and the leader."[31] Demonstrating KJI's ability to successfully handle the nuclear crisis was a crucial goal for the North Korea government, which had staged several big events—the fortieth anniversary of the end of the Korean War and eighty-one-year-old KIS's birthday. Before the UN Security Council took action by issuing a presidential statement in March 1994, North Korea stepped up exercises of offensive and defensive forces, mobilized its population by staging a mass rally, and held a conference of party cells.

In a similar fashion, KJU has the burden of demonstrating his ability to manage challenges. While the confrontation between North Korea and the international community over stopping missile and nuclear tests continued, North Koreans attended a rally where they declared to be ready to fire long-range nuclear-armed missiles at the United States.[32] North Korean army officers chanted slogans during a rally at Kim Il Sung Square to protest against toughened UN sanctions against North Korea, and similar events continued when North Korea announced the cancellation of the nonaggression pact and nuclear disarmament agreements with South Korea. In this way, North Korea's leadership values "face saving" and took a defiant stance to avoid appearing weak to its people.

The KJU regime announced that 2012 would mark the watershed moment of transforming North Korea into a "strong and prosperous nation." It has conducted symbolic actions to showcase its technological prowess by launching missiles and conducting a nuclear test. Since North Korea could not make a decisive improvement in economic sectors, it had to turn domestic attention to something grandiose: North Korea put a greater focus on research and development in technology and science by building houses for scientists who were involved in missile and nuclear tests and holding ceremonial events to praise advancement in missile- and nuclear-related technology.[33] North Korea's dilemma is that the means of countering internal challenges is the cause of external challenges. Given that every important decision inevitably involves a trade-off, North Korea's foreign policy decision making also involves evaluation of preferred options and alternatives.

Influence of Political Doctrine and Culture-of-Honor Norm. North Korea's domestic ideology is one of the primary forces driving its actions. Because the legitimacy of the regime had been built on Juche ideology, North Korea exercised principles of its political ideology rather than internalizing the norms shared by the other members of the international system. Juche, known as "self-reliance," means "autonomy" and indicates that North Korea determines the fate of the nation.[34] KJI suggested impending tasks to infuse Juche spirit in every part of society. The suggestion was adopted as an official party line at the 6th KWP convention in 1980. He proposed three principles of North Korea's policy—*jaju* (self-determination) in politics, *jarip* (self-sufficiency) in economy, and *jawi* (self-defense) in national defense—that have evolved from Juche ideology and share common features. Such principles have also directed North Korea's behavior in its relationship with others. Like his father and his grandfather, KJU utilizes this Juche idea as a political doctrine to arouse nationalistic drive among North Koreans.

As a strategy to realize its self-determination, North Korea often mentions the central-link (*jungshimgori*) strategy, which refers to something that is the most important part of any problem and therefore becomes the key aspect that can resolve the whole complicated situation. It seems that North Korea views the nuclear weapons capability as a key opportunity to resolve both economic and political issues. By signing the Geneva Agreed Framework, North Korea intended to resolve multiple issues—ensuring energy supply, diplomatic recognition by the United States and elimination of threats to its regime.[35] By withdrawing from the NPT, North Korea claimed to exercise "just and revolutionary measures to save the entire nation from the peril of war and protect dignity of the nation."[36] North Korea's determination to pursue simultaneous development of its economy and nuclear weapons capability by declaring a new policy line of parallel economic construction and nuclear weapons development is another application of this strategy.

Equality is a significant component of Juche ideology, and the principle of reciprocity is applied to its foreign relations.[37] The North Korea nuclear issue was understood by the international community as a problem caused by Pyongyang. However, North Korea viewed the nuclear issue as an interconnected matter to be resolved by both sides. During the first nuclear crisis, North Korea asserted that the delay in nuclear negotiation originated from Washington's ignorance of the principle of mutual respect and its lack of will to implement agreements simultaneously.[38] During the second nuclear crisis, North Korea stressed a reciprocal relation in line with the principle of commitment for commitment and action for action, while the United States insisted on realizing denuclearization first and establishing a peace regime later. North Korea reasoned that its nuclear test was aimed at attracting international attention to consolidate its image as a nuclear weapons state and enhance its status as an equal partner of the nuclear talks.

North Korea has held on to the traditional concept of sovereign right as a principle of foreign policy. They perceive the concept of sovereignty in terms of noninterference rather than membership and reasonably good standing in the international community. The country's leadership considers imposed demands to be an extraordinary infringement of its sovereign rights.[39] For North Korea, defeating threats caused by the nuclear crisis can be understood as a means to ensure sovereignty, and overcoming the crisis in a creative fashion serves the goal of realizing self-determination. Warning that the United States would be responsible for all the measures taken by North Korea, Pyongyang rationalized a "struggle" against any attempt to threaten its sovereign right.[40] All of these suggest that North Korea's decision making stemming from culture-of-honor norms is part of its foreign policy.

CONCLUSION

This study tries to examine how North Korea's unique political culture and ideology shapes North Korea's identity and interests in order to better explain its interactions with the international community. It also explains the significance of understanding how the competitive environment guided North Korea's noncooperative behavior and how a fixed negative image led to deepening of North Korea's defiant actions. Traditionally, states joining the international community are expected to internalize the norms shared by members within the system. However, in a controlled place like North Korea, domestically endorsed values are more likely to affect North Korea's nuclear policy decision making.[41] Isolation of North Korea from the international community and negative relations with other countries let leadership stress an exclusive concept of sovereignty. Because North Korea policy was formulated as a response to external threats to the maintenance of Juche-oriented socialism, the more the crisis intensified, the more North Korea sought solutions in consolidating internal unity and pursuing guiding principles.[42]

Because a state's perception of the others is of a historical construction, North Korea's unexpected signals of "forming an atmosphere for the improvement of North-South relations" in the form of KJU's annual New Year's Day speech[43] and subsequent peace offensive do not seem to be convincing the international community. Washington and Seoul unite in demanding that North Korea take concrete actions, not merely show the direction of its policy. It is important to understand that North Korea has shifted between revisionist and status-quo power. Since North Korea faces the challenges of uniting the people, generating rents sought by the elites, and lifting obstacles to earn hard currency, reconciliatory measures could be highly valued in the minds of the new leadership in the North. Nonetheless, the peace offensive can also be understood within the context of a grand scheme—to safeguard Juche socialism. Hence, it remains to be seen whether the recent peaceful gestures can be fully materialized.

NOTES

1. Richard N. Rosecrance, "British Incentives to Become a Nuclear Power," in *The Dispersion of Nuclear Weapons*, ed. Richard N. Rosecrance (New York: Columbia University Press, 1964).

2. Robert F. Goheen, "Problems of Proliferation: US Policy and the Third World," *World Politics* 35, no. 2 (1983): 194–215.

3. William Epstein, "Why States Go—And Don't Go—Nuclear," *Annals AAPSS* 430 (March 1977): 16–38.

4. William R. Van Cleave and Harold W. Rood, "Spread of Nuclear Weapons," *Military Review* 46 (December 1966): 3–10.

5. Robert Keohane, "The Big Influence of Small Allies," *Foreign Policy* 1 (1971): 162–3.

6. T. V. Paul, *Power versus Prudence: Why Nations Forgo Nuclear Weapons* (Montreal: McGill-Queen's University Press, 2000).

7. Alexander Wendt, "Collective Identity Formation and the International State," *American Political Science Review* 88, no. 2 (1994): 384–96.

8. For example, during the political turmoil under the regime of President Rhee Syngman, who declared martial law and jailed members of parliament leading to a student uprising, and under the military rule of President Park Chung Hee, who promulgated an emergency decree causing popular unrest. North Korea attempted high-profile provocations including the unsuccessful assassination of President Park, the hijacking of a Korean Airlines F-27 plane, and the digging of an infiltration tunnel across the DMZ (the demilitarized zone).

9. DPRK Constitution, Preamble.

10. DPRK Constitution, Art. 17.

11. Kyedong Kim, *North Korea's Foreign Policy* (Seoul: Baeksanseodang, 2002).

12. North Korea's ideology, Juche, means exercising autonomy.

13. DPRK Constitution, Art. 37, para. 2.

14. DPRK Constitution, Art. 55, para. 1.

15. Kongdan Oh and Ralph C. Hassig, *North Korea through the Looking Glass* (Washington, DC: Brookings Institution Press, 2000), 192.

16. "N. Korea might give up its military nation identity by shifting to party-first policy" [in Korean], *Dong-A Ilbo*, 27 August 2013.

17. Charter of Korean Workers' Party.

18. Herbert C. Kelman, "Compliance, Identification, and Internalization: Three Processes of Attitude Change," *Journal of Conflict Resolution* 2, no. 1 (1958): 53.

19. Wendt argues that a state with a corporate identity pursues selfish interests rather than collective interests in a condition where fear is great. Wendt, "Collective Identity Formation and the International State."

20. Constructivists contend that a state's corporate identity is the intrinsic qualities that constitute actor individuality, and this aspect of identity is based on domestic politics. Ronald L. Jepperson, Alexander Wendt, and Peter J. Katzenstein, "Norms, Identity, and Culture in National Security," in *The*

Culture of National Security: Norms and Identity in World Politics, ed. Peter J. Katzenstein (New York: Columbia University Press, 1996), 50.

21. Moon Young Huh, *Characteristics of North Korea's Diplomacy and Prospect of Change* (Seoul: Korea Institute of National Unification, 2001), 3.

22. Jina Kim, *The North Korean Nuclear Weapons Crisis* (New York: Palgrave McMillan, 2014).

23. Dae Sook Suh, *Kim Il Sung: The North Korean Leader*, 2nd ed. (New York: Columbia University Press, 1995), 115.

24. "The US IS an Evil Empire," *Rodong Shinmun*, 14 February 2002.

25. "Request for the US to Take Practical Actions to Implement the Agreed Framework," *KCNA*, 3 March 2000.

26. "We Should Repel Ideological and Cultural Infiltration of Imperialism" *Rodong Shinmun*, 1 June 1999.

27. Selig Harrison, *Korean Endgame: A Strategy for Reunification and US Disengagement* (Princeton: Princeton University Press, 2002), 70.

28. "US Pirate Ship Arrived at Busan Port," *KCNA*, 24 August 1998.

29. "With You, We Can Win," *Rodong Shinmun*, 16 February 1994.

30. Jina Kim, "UN Sanctions as an Instrument of Coercive Diplomacy against North Korea," paper presented at the Brookings Institute, Washington, DC, 5 September 2013.

31. "North Korea Holds Conference of Secretaries of Party Cell," *Hankyoreh*, 27 March 1993, 2.

32. Corky Siemaszko, "North Korea Threatens Nuke Attack on US before the UN Slaps the Country with Tough Sanctions," *New York Daily News*, 7 March 2013.

33. Ilgun Yoon, "Kim Jong Un, Visited Construction Site of Building Apartment for Kim Il Sung University Scientists," *Yonhap News*, 14 August 2013.

34. Jae Jin Seo, *New Analysis of the Construction and Change of Juche Ideology* (Seoul: KINU Press, 2001).

35. Charles Pritchard, F*ailed Diplomacy: The Tragic Story of How North Korea Got the Bomb* (Washington, DC: Brookings Institute, 2007), 119.

36. "Protest against Resolution on Special Inspection," *Hankyoreh*, 15 March 1993.

37. Woosang Kim, "In Dealing with a Hawkish Rival: Game Theoretic and Empirical Analyses of the Korean Peninsula Case," *Korean Journal of Defense Analysis* 14, no. 2 (2002): 29–50.

38. "Nuclear Issue on the Korean Peninsula Can Be Resolved by Dialogue, Not by Pressure," *Rodong Shinmun*, 12 November 1993.

39. "Legitimacy of Independent Foreign Policy of the Korean Worker's Party," *Rodong Shinmun*, 28 August 2002.

40. "Realizing Autonomy of Our Nation is the Basis of Being the Master of Our Destiny," *Rodong Shinmun*, 2 July 1998.

41. Dennis Chong, *Rational Lives: Norms and Values in Politics and Society* (Chicago: University of Chicago Press, 2000), 148.

42. Chol U Kim, *Songun Politics of Kim Il Sung* (Pyongyang: Foreign Languages Publishing House, 2002), 11–12.

43. Choe Sang Hun, "North Korean Leader Says He Wants Better Ties with South," *New York Times*, 31 December 2013.

CHAPTER 2

North Korea's Nuclear Development, the Non-Proliferation Treaty Regime, and Regional Security

Shinichi OGAWA

Almost immediately after its conclusion of a comprehensive safeguards agreement with the International Atomic Energy Agency (IAEA), the Democratic People's Republic of Korea (DPRK) defiantly began challenging the IAEA authority and has kept an illicit nuclear weapons program despite mounting pressure from the international community. This chapter first describes responses taken by the IAEA and the UN Security Council (UNSC) vis-à-vis North Korea and suggests a couple of lessons obtained from experiences dealing with the North's weapons program. The latter half of this study explores whether there is still a prospect for denuclearizing North Korea. Finally this essay analyzes the potential strategic impact North Korea's nuclear weapons have on the regional security. The central argument of this chapter is that nuclear nonproliferation is not attainable simply through the existing nonproliferation measures and procedures; it requires a degree of conformity in strategic interests among the states concerned and political cooperation among them.

IMPACT OF NORTH KOREA'S BEHAVIOR ON THE NUCLEAR NON-PROLIFERATION TREATY (NPT)

Noncompliance with the IAEA Safeguards

North Korea's attempt to extract weapons-grade plutonium and develop nuclear weapons, stretching over two decades, has undermined the credibility and reliability of the NPT-IAEA regime and the UNSC. North Korea successfully frustrated the IAEA's verification efforts and evaded the IAEA safeguards. After the DPRK submitted its initial report to the IAEA in May 1992 under the IAEA-DPRK safeguards agreement, ad hoc inspections by IAEA to verify Pyongyang's statement began. Shortly thereafter inconsistencies emerged between the North's initial declaration and the agency's findings. The mismatch suggested that there existed undeclared plutonium in North Korea. In February 1993 the IAEA Director General invoked the "special inspection" procedure and requested the North to accept that inspection to clarify the inconsistency.[1] The DPRK refused the request. In April 1993 the IAEA Board of Governors concluded that the DPRK was in noncompliance with the IAEA-DPRK safeguards agreement and referred this noncompliance to the UNSC. In May 1993 the Security Council adopted Resolution 825 calling upon the DPRK to comply with its safeguards agreement,[2] but it was to no avail. The special inspection did not take place.

Theoretically, under the NPT, a state-party to the treaty can develop sensitive nuclear technologies (e.g., technologies for uranium enrichment and reprocessing of spent nuclear fuel) in a way that does not infringe the letter of the NPT, and then withdraw from the NPT to acquire weapons-grade nuclear materials and weaponize them as a non-party. Though this loophole is one important weakness of the NPT, North Korea did not exploit this shortcoming. What North Korea did was to repeatedly defy the IAEA authority and to violate the IAEA-DPRK comprehensive safeguards agreement. The failure of the IAEA and the UNSC to make Pyongyang compliant with nonproliferation obligations has generated a serious credibility and reliability problem for the NPT-IAEA regime.

North Korea's Withdrawal from the NPT and Pursuit of Nuclear Weapons

Another challenge North Korea has posed to the reliability of the NPT is its trouble-free withdrawal from the NPT. On 12 March 1993 North Korea, rejecting IAEA's request for a special inspection, announced its decision to withdraw from the NPT. The DPRK is the first state-party to announced departure from the treaty,[3] though it later put the withdrawal on hold.[4]

Like many other international treaties, the NPT contains a withdrawal clause, which stipulates that any state-party to the treaty has the right to withdraw if it decides that "extraordinary events, related to the subject matter of this Treaty, have jeopardized the supreme interests of its country."[5] The clause requires the withdrawing state to "give notice of such withdrawal" not only to all other parties to the NPT but also to the UNSC three months in advance with a statement of its reasons for withdrawal. This provision is intended to give the Security Council an opportunity to deal with any withdrawal that may bring about a threat to international peace and security.

In May 1993, two months after North Korea's declaration of withdrawal from the NPT, the UNSC adopted Resolution 825, calling upon the DPRK to "reconsider the announcement" of withdrawal and to "reaffirm its commitment to the Treaty."[6] But the resolution did not make reference to any sanctions if North Korea failed to comply with the Security Council nor decided whether Pyongyang should be permitted to withdraw from the NPT.

On 10 January 2003 the NPT-noncompliant DPRK announced an immediate withdrawal from the NPT by revoking the June 1993 "suspension" on the effectuation of its withdrawal from the NPT.[7] However, no agreed statement on the matter was issued by the UNSC. The UNSC simply expressed its "concern" over the situation in North Korea and said it would keep following developments there.[8] The UNSC's inaction allowed North Korea to continue with its nuclear weapons program, and on 10 February 2005 North Korea announced the possession of nuclear weapons. It was not until October 2006 that the Security Council responded with penalties to Pyongyang's withdrawal from the NPT and its illicit nuclear weapons program by adopting Resolution 1718,[9] enacting a variety of multilateral nonmilitary sanctions. Resolution 1718 was largely motivated by Pyongyang's first nuclear test conducted on 9 October 2006. Nonetheless, as North

Korea's behavior thereafter shows, neither the Security Council's sanctions mandated by Resolution 1718, nor the additional Resolutions 1874 (June 2009) and 2087 (January 2013) were successful in compelling Pyongyang to give up its nuclear weapons and return to the NPT.

One important reason for the insufficient level of the UNSC sanctions can be found in China's half-hearted support for the punishments against Pyongyang. For geopolitical reasons North Korea's only ally China consistently prioritized North Korea's political stability—in practical terms, the survival of the regime—over its denuclearization. Therefore, before UNSC Resolution 2094 (March 2013), China tried to dilute and soften the contents of UN sanctions, sometimes hinting it might employ its veto power, for fear that severe economic and other nonmilitary punishments might destabilize North Korea. Considering that the UNSC already declared in January 1992 that the proliferation of weapons of mass destruction (WMD) is a threat to international peace and security,[10] China should have been more in line with the other Security Council members in punishing the DPRK's violations of the NPT system and its illicit nuclear weapons development.

Owing to the lack of effective countermeasures against Pyongyang's noncompliance with the IAEA-DPRK safeguards agreement and withdrawal from the NPT, North Korea succeeded in fabricating primitive nuclear explosive devices and has been able to work toward smaller and lighter nuclear warheads that can be mated with its ballistic missiles.[11] The case of the DPRK reveals vividly the deficiencies and weakness of the NPT-IAEA regime and also the UNSC, which often suffers from divisive geopolitical interests among the permanent members. Pyongyang's actions may have set a precedent that will further erode the current nuclear nonproliferation regime. Other NPT non-nuclear states in similar situations may calculate that, as Pyongyang has done, they can endure the political and economic costs incurred by their own potential pursuit of nuclear weapons.

Fueling Nuclear Proliferation

Pyongyang's nuclear weapons program has provided cash-hungry North Korea with chances to earn hard currency by exporting nuclear materials and technologies for producing weapons-grade nuclear materials, thereby fostering nuclear proliferation worldwide. It is reported that North Korea supplied in 2000 about 1.7 tons of uranium hexafluoride to Libya.[12] Similarly, the DPRK allegedly assisted Syria's covert nuclear reactor program.[13] Pyongyang's record of transferring nuclear materials and technology to nuclear aspirants constitutes a direct threat to the NPT regime.

DEALING WITH THE WEAKNESS OF THE NPT-IAEA REGIME

Along with Iraq's covert attempt to acquire weapons-grade fissile materials, North Korea's refusal to accept IAEA's special inspection clearly illustrated the limits of the IAEA's comprehensive safeguards activities. In order to deal with this problem, the IAEA in 1997 formulated an Additional Protocol to a comprehensive safeguards agreement. This Additional Protocol has enabled the IAEA to obtain supplementary information about nuclear activities of non-nuclear weapon states (NNWSs) and to get access to undeclared nuclear materials and nuclear-related sites located in those states.

However, the IAEA cannot compel non-nuclear parties to the NPT to accede to the Protocol. For a measure to mitigate this problem, in June 2011 the Nuclear Suppliers Group revised their guidelines for exports of sensitive enrichment and reprocessing items and technologies and has mandated that the member states should require the conclusion and implementation not only of a comprehensive safeguards agreement but also of an Additional Protocol with the IAEA as a condition for new supply arrangements with NNWSs.[14] The amendment is expected to promote NNWSs to agree to an Additional Protocol when they plan to accelerate their civilian nuclear developments. Yet, NNWSs that do not abandon the nuclear weapon option would not accede to the IAEA Additional Protocol. Technology is destined to diffuse, and a determined proliferator like North Korea would attempt to acquire enrichment and reprocessing items and technologies through any means available.

Another noteworthy approach to preventing NNWSs from acquiring weapons-grade nuclear materials is the multilateral nuclear approach (MNA), which involves applying multinational alternatives to the national operation of uranium-enrichment and plutonium-separation technologies and to the disposal of spent nuclear fuel. This approach had been discussed in the Cold War days and was revisited by IAEA Director General Mohamed ElBaradei in 2003. Nonetheless, MNAs have failed so far to materialize outside Europe due to different political and economic perceptions among NNWSs in the other regions.

It is often argued that the success of the nuclear nonproliferation regime depends not merely upon supply-side approaches such as strengthening IAEA's verification capability and export controls, but also upon demand-side approaches, typical of which are negative and positive security assurances to NNWSs.[15] The NPT-permitted nuclear weapon states (NWSs) have long declared conditional (the United States, the United Kingdom, France, and Russia) or unconditional (China) negative security assurances, and non-nuclear Non-Aligned Movement states have persistently requested that negative assurances be put in a stronger and legally binding form. Yet, it is dubious that legally binding negative security assurances are more credible and reliable than the current political assurances, in view of the fact that assurances are by nature unverifiable. The doubt has been reinforced by Russia's seizure of Crimea from Ukraine in March 2014 in violation of the Budapest Memorandum of December 1994.[16] Extended nuclear deterrence (nuclear umbrella) provided by a NWS is one type of positive security assurance and generally is considered to be more effective than negative security assurances,[17] but the scope of such undertaking cannot be worldwide. In addition, relying too much on nuclear deterrence in itself is not compatible with nuclear nonproliferation norms. Moreover, security assurances cannot address all motivations for going nuclear; security assurances do not work for NNWSs that attempt to acquire nuclear weapons for regional hegemony or national prestige.

On the other hand, timely and credible responses to noncompliances and effective enforcement mechanisms to remedy them are no less helpful for strengthening the NPT-IAEA regime than the supply-side and demand-side approaches. Indeed, in deterring state-parties from abetting proliferation and preventing an NPT-noncompliant state from withdrawing from the NPT, a strong likelihood of severe nonmilitary sanctions and, if necessary, military actions through the UNSC is indispensable. The UNSC up to now has not always functioned as expected. In the case of North Korea, China, as already mentioned, has steadfastly opposed the adoption of harsh sanctions against North Korea for geopolitical reasons. China's lukewarm attitude toward North Korea's nuclear problem has resulted in the greatest difficulty in deterring Pyongyang from violating its nonproliferation obligations and from ignoring legally binding Security Council resolutions.

In order to mitigate this type of problem, Pierre Goldschmidt has proposed that the UNSC adopt a generic, non-state-specific resolution dealing preventively with cases of both noncompliance and NPT withdrawal. In a case of noncompliance, the generic resolution provides that the UNSC would automatically adopt a specific resolution under Chapter VII of the UN Charter requiring the noncompliant state to grant the IAEA expanded access rights beyond what is granted under a comprehensive safeguards agreement and an Additional Protocol. In dealing with the withdrawal from the NPT by a noncompliant state-party, the UNSC, under Chapter VII of the UN Charter, adopts another preventive and legally binding resolution to the effect that withdrawal notice by an NPT-noncompliant state constitutes a threat to international peace and security, with all the punitive consequences that may follow.[18] As Goldschmidt argues, an advance agreement by the Security Council on a set of standard responses to be applied evenhandedly to any noncompliant state, regardless of its relations with a permanent member of the Security Council, would significantly enhance the credibility of the nonproliferation regime. The UNSC Resolution 1540 of April 2004 that intends to cope with proliferation of WMD to non-state actors is one example of such a legally binding, preventive, and generic UNSC resolution under Chapter VII of the UN Charter. The UN member states have to urge the members of the UNSC, the permanent five in particular, to come together and attain political will to adopt such a resolution in order to strengthen the nuclear nonproliferation regime.

COORDINATED ACTIONS FOR ROLLING BACK PYONGYANG'S NUCLEAR PROGRAM?

North Korea has long extracted weapons-grade plutonium and is now making efforts to weaponize its nuclear explosive devices.[19] Any measures taken in the future to strengthen the NPT-IAEA regime are no longer helpful for denuclearizing North Korea. What policy options are left for the international community, in particular for the five states (the United States, South Korea, China, Russia, and Japan) of the Six-Party Talks?

Some may argue for launching a surgical air strike against Pyongyang's nuclear facilities,[20] as Israel did vis-à-vis Iraq in June 1981 and Syria in September 2007. However, there is almost no prospect for a military solution to the North's nuclear development. Bombing North Korea's nuclear facilities, which already house nuclear and radioactive materials, would most likely cause environmental hazards that would hurt innocent North Korean people. In addition, given the paranoid and impetuous nature of North Korea's leadership, any military strike on the DPRK is likely to invite Pyongyang's counterattack on Seoul, resulting in devastation of the city. For this reason South Korea has never supported and will not support such military action. On top of that, the feasibility of a military solution would diminish over time, since North Korea is advancing toward attaining a nuclear-armed missile capability. Moreover, a military solution such as an air strike would not be an ultimate solution; it can at best only delay the acquisition of nuclear weapons by a determined proliferator, as shown by Saddam Hussein's resumption of his clandestine nuclear development after the Israeli air strike against Iraq's nuclear reactor.

On the other hand, there is a view that the United States and other members of the international community should find ways to live with a nuclear-armed North Korea. The argument is based both on past experiences that include the failure of several rounds of sanctions to compel the DPRK to relinquish its nuclear weapons and also on the fear that the current North Korea policies of Seoul and Washington risk creating a scenario in which a nuclear-armed North Korea, convinced that its adversaries are determined to destroy it, may launch a desperate, live-or-die counterblow in a dire crisis.[21] However, recognizing North Korea, an NPT-noncompliant and the only state that has withdrawn from it, as a nuclear-armed state is a nightmare for the NPT-IAEA regime since such a concession seriously erodes the credibility and reliability of the regime. Thus it is better to examine once again if there remains any room for persuading Pyongyang to give up its nuclear weapons.

Analyzing North Korea's motivation for developing nuclear weapons can guide us. First, the North's leadership appears to believe that nuclear weapons serve as an effective deterrent against US and South Korea's military intervention and as a means for preventing foreign domination and interference. The North Korean elite may believe that Saddam Hussein might still be living in his palace today had he successfully developed nuclear weapons. Second, by having nuclear weapons, North Korea can grab the attention of the international community and extort economic assistance from its neighboring states and the United States. Nuclear blackmail is an effective way for Pyongyang to maintain its failing economy. Third, North Korea may well believe that nuclear weapons serve as an important tool to consolidate support within its military. Such thinking may have been fostered by poor economic conditions and difficulties caused by UN sanctions in acquiring advanced conventional weapons from foreign countries. Fourth, the North Korean regime needs the prestige of nuclear weapons status to balance against rival South Korea's enormous economic successes. All of these purported motives, apart from the third one, are susceptible to engagement and actions by other states.

In order to persuade Pyongyang to give up nuclear weapons, whether through sticks, carrots, or any other means, more extensive collaboration and greater policy consistency among the five countries of the Six-Party Talks are absolutely essential. In the past the absence of a united front and policy consistency among the five partner countries often created an environment of indecisiveness, allowing the North Korean regime to effectively exploit policy differences among the five countries. While the US administration under George W. Bush was listing North Korea as one of the "axis of evil" states, South Korea's Kim Dae Jung and Roh Moo Hyun governments were providing Pyongyang with helping hands through the "Sunshine Policy." While the United States, South Korea, Russia, and Japan were implementing economic and trade sanctions mandated by UNSC resolutions, North Korea's only ally China was supportive of North Korea and provided much-needed economic assistance, despite Pyongyang's failure to comply with UNSC resolutions calling for it to dismantle its nuclear and ballistic missile programs. It is even reported that China's trade with North Korea increased in the aftermath of UN sanctions against North Korea.[22]

Glyn Davies, the US special representative for North Korea policy, said in June 2013 that Washington had not tried a "concerted multilateral effort" that should have sent "common signals" to Pyongyang from the United States,

South Korea, China, Russia, and Japan. He declared that the United States has now put higher priority on efforts to coordinate with partner countries so that they speak with "one voice" before negotiating with Pyongyang on denuclearization.[23] When sticks and sanctions against the North are deemed necessary, as it stands today, it is indispensable for the United States, South Korea, Russia, and Japan to encourage China to pursue a more concerted North Korea policy.

The US policy adjustment appeared to be facilitated by China's unprecedented tough stance toward Pyongyang after its third nuclear test conducted in February 2013. Immediately after the test, China's then–Foreign Minister Yang Jiechi summoned the North Korean ambassador in Beijing and protested sternly, saying China was "strongly dissatisfied and resolutely opposed" to the test, and urged North Korea to "stop any rhetoric or acts that could worsen situations and return to the right course of dialogue and consultation as soon as possible."[24] In condemning Pyongyang's nuclear testing, China voted in favor of UNSC Resolution 2094, which tightened financial sanctions by making mandatory some of the existing measures. In addition Beijing agreed, in a departure from the previous sanctions, to make obligatory the interdiction and inspection of all suspicious ships and cargo en route to or from North Korea.

Indeed, North Korea's continued nuclear and ballistic missile developments and provocative actions jeopardize China's national security interests. First, China arguably does not want to see neighboring North Korea, a country difficult to rein in and unstable by nature, armed with nuclear-capable ballistic missiles. Second, North Korea's attempt to acquire nuclear-armed long-range missiles has stimulated the United States to upgrade its homeland ballistic missile defense capability, which can damage China's strategic deterrent vis-à-vis the United States. The Obama administration decided to augment its missile-interceptors for homeland defense from thirty to forty-four[25] after Pyongyang's launch of a long-range rocket in December 2012. Third, North Korea's nuclear and ballistic missile developments and provocative actions contribute to the strengthening of the US alliance system in Northeast Asia that Beijing considers a tool of encirclement of China.

Having said that, it is still not clear whether China is ready to impose heavy and harsh sanctions that may risk inviting the downfall of the North Korean regime. China cannot afford to risk disorder and chaos in North

Korea. This would not only be likely to generate destabilizing effects on the China-DPRK border but also would cause a serious confrontation with the United States and South Korea over the political settlement of a post-Kim North Korea. More importantly, strategic and political trends in East Asia decrease the likelihood that Beijing will dramatically alter its North Korea policy. The Chinese leadership appears to consider ongoing US rebalancing toward Asia as a policy of containing China. Furthermore, China has incited an intractable territorial issue with Japan.[26] These fundamental Chinese security issues will not evaporate even if North Korea is denuclearized or its regime is ended.[27] Thus China's North Korea policy will be a measured one, as it has been, balancing delicately between assisting North Korea's survival by maintaining a certain level of economic and trade interactions with the protégé regime while at the same time trying to curb Pyongyang's nuclear ambitions. In short, there is little chance for the United States, South Korea, and Japan to see China's North Korea policy change into a more coordinated one and to expect denuclearization of North Korea in the foreseeable future.

REGIONAL STRATEGIC IMPACT
OF A NUCLEAR NORTH KOREA

At present, North Korea does not seem to have a lighter and smaller bomb design that it can confidently mount on a missile.[28] Yet, sooner or later Pyongyang will be able to acquire such design either through foreign assistance or its own technological development. According to the 2010 "Ballistic Missile Defense Review," the US government estimates that short of a drastic change in DPRK security strategy, North Korea "will be able to mate a nuclear warhead to a proven delivery system" within the next decade.[29]

However, even if the North attains a capability of equipping its ballistic missiles with nuclear warheads, the likelihood of North Korea launching a nuclear first strike against South Korea, Japan, or the United States is very low. This is simply because Pyongyang's use of nuclear weapons against these countries is very likely to invite military retaliation that would ensure the destruction or collapse of North Korean regime—and regime survival is Pyongyang's most important reason for building nuclear weapons. Thus, unless the neighboring states drive the North into a corner and put it on the verge of collapse, the North would not dare to use nuclear weapons first.

Nevertheless, a nuclear-armed North Korea may increase the risk of a skirmish that, in the worst case, might inadvertently escalate into a large-scale conventional war. Pyongyang may believe that its nuclear arsenal gives it more freedom to conduct limited military provocations, such as the 2010 sinking of a South Korean naval ship or the Yeonpyeong Island shelling, without reprisal. In order to respond to such provocations, however, South Korea is reported to be planning to launch "preventive attacks" if the North is preparing for another limited strike.[30] Such a military response by Seoul may lead to a rapid escalation of hostilities. Should a large-scale military clash occur on the Peninsula and the North believes its regime is on the brink of collapse, Pyongyang is likely to use its surviving nuclear-armed missiles, since at that stage there would be nothing left for the leadership to lose. In such a dire situation, deterrence would break down.

To keep North Korea from resorting to the use of nuclear weapons during a conventional war, the United States and South Korea do not have any effective countermeasures except for, at an early stage of military escalation, launching preemptive counterforce strikes against the North's missiles, missile sites, and long-range artillery pieces targeting Seoul. It is doubtful, however, whether such a counterforce attack would be successful, since it is not easy to destroy mobile missiles, and most of the North's ballistic missiles are on mobile launchers.[31] In short, military provocation and miscalculation by a nuclear-armed North Korea would lead to its demise and, in the worst case, might bring about a nuclear disaster on South Korea and Japan.

There are some concerns that North Korea's nuclear activities would drive South Korea or Japan to reconsider their non-nuclear status.[32] The two countries have civilian nuclear power programs and technical expertise that can be oriented toward nuclear weapons development. Yet it is unlikely that Pyongyang's nuclear weapons per se would hasten the nuclearization of the two countries. So long as the US extended nuclear deterrence covering South Korea and Japan is considered reasonably credible, both South Korea and Japan see no need to pursue their own nuclear weapons capabilities. On the military side, the credibility of the US nuclear umbrella is buttressed by overwhelming US nuclear capabilities, powerful and second-to-none counterforce capability in particular. On the political side, the US–South

Korea and US-Japan alliances are intact today, and no significant event has occurred that might lead a third party to conclude that the two alliances are on the verge of breakdown. Thus it is unrealistic and wrong to assume that South Korea or Japan no longer has faith in the US nuclear umbrella vis-à-vis North Korea. Furthermore, South Korean or Japanese nuclear capability would add little to deter a DPRK nuclear attack. It is true that there are several possible scenarios in which US nuclear forces could not deter a North Korea nuclear use against South Korea or Japan: an unauthorized nuclear launch, an irrational decision by the leadership to employ nuclear weapons, or a final act of desperation by a regime about to collapse. These scenarios of nuclear weapons usage by Pyongyang could not be deterred by any means, including not only US, but also South Korean or Japanese nuclear weapons.

Moreover, nuclear acquisition by South Korea or Japan would fuel North Korea's nuclear development, making any future nonproliferation accord with Pyongyang much harder to reach. In addition, Japanese nuclearization would further aggravate Japan's relations with South Korea and China, which have not forgotten Japanese aggression before and during World War II. In short, loss of confidence in US nuclear guarantees, not Pyongyang's nuclear weapons development, might prove to be the crucial tipping point convincing South Korea's and Japan's defense planners to go nuclear.

CONCLUSION

North Korea will continue to survive UN sanctions and international pressure and keep on developing nuclear weapon capabilities. What policy options remain for the international community to deal with this intractable problem? As already mentioned, unless it is cornered a nuclear-armed Pyongyang will not dare to use its nuclear weapons first, though it may be more prone to make minor provocations that might involve conventional weapons. Thus the international community has time to launch the following policy mix, which may take a long time to bear fruit.

First, the international community should make Pyongyang's nuclear development a long and costly process. Given the remaining technical challenges facing Pyongyang such as fabricating small and lighter nuclear warheads and reliable re-entry vehicles, attaining a militarily significant nuclear weapons capability will demand time, expertise, and a great deal of resources. The international community should work as much as possible to limit Pyongyang's access to crucial materials and technology.

Second and in parallel with the aforementioned, the United States, South Korea, China, Russia, and Japan should engage North Korean citizens patiently and launch various measures that can help the North Korean people access outside information so as to encourage internal change in North Korea's society. Deepening engagement is a promising way to facilitate a gradual and positive change in North Korea. The North Korean people have long suffered from a brutal tyranny imposed by the Kim family. If history is any guide, dictators eventually fall from power, driven out by their own people who discover the reality of the outside world or are no longer able to endure their suffering.

Third, China must be convinced that denuclearizing North Korea and transforming it into a normal state is as much conducive to its security as maintaining the status quo and the stability of North Korea. China should consider the defiant, impetuous, and nuclear-armed North Korea as a security problem not only for the other regional states, but also for itself. For China, today's North Korea is a liability rather than a strategic asset. The long-claimed geopolitical value of North Korea as a buffer state for China is diminishing in the current age of air power. And what is worse, North Korea may draw China into a regional conflict that China does not want to get involved in. If China continues to be unable to rein in its protégé, doubts would rise in the international community about whether China, which is set to establish a great-power relationship with the United States in Asia and the Pacific, really can act like a responsible regional leader.

NOTES

1. IAEA, "Fact Sheet on DPRK Nuclear Safeguards," http://www.iaea.org /newscenter/focus/iaeadprk/fact_sheet_may2003.shtml.

2. United Nations Security Council, Resolution 825 (UNSCR825), 11 May 1993, http://daccess-dds-ny.un.org/doc/UNDOC/GEN/N93/280/49/IMG /N9328049.pdf?OpenElement.

3. However, some NPT parties, including the three depositories of the treaty, questioned whether Pyongyang's stated reasons for withdrawing from the Treaty constitute any "extraordinary events" that "jeopardized the supreme interests" of North Korea. See UNSCR825.

4. On 11 June 1993, one day before the coming into effect of its withdrawal, the DPRK declared to "unilaterally suspend" the effectuation of its withdrawal in a US-DPRK joint statement issued on the same day.

5. See paragraph 1 of Article X of the NPT.

6. UNSCR825.

7. S/2003/91, 27 January 2003, Annex I. North Korea said its withdrawal was immediate since Pyongyang suspended its withdrawal from the NPT in June 1993 just one day before it was to take effect after reaching an agreement with the United States.

8. IAEA, "Fact Sheet on DPRK Nuclear Safeguards."

9. http://www.un.org/en/ga/search/view_doc.asp?symbol=S/RES/1718(2006).

10. Note by the President of the Security Council, 31 January 1992, http:// daccess-dds-ny.un.org/doc/UNDOC/GEN/N92/043/34/PDF/N9204334 .pdf?OpenElement.

11. Terence Roehrig, "North Korea's Nuclear Weapons: Future Strategy and Doctrine." *Policy Brief*, Harvard University, May 2013, http://belfercenter .hks.harvard.edu/publication/23074/north_koreas_nuclear_weapons.html ?breadcrumb=%2Fpublication%2Fby_type%2Fpolicy_brief.

12. Olli Heinonen, "North Korean Nuclear Program in Transition," 6 March 2012, http://belfercenter.ksg.harvard.edu/files/nuke.pdf. Uranium hexa-fluoride (UF_6) is a chemical compound consisting of one atom of uranium combined with six atoms of fluorine. It is the chemical form of uranium that is used during the uranium-enrichment process. Within a reasonable range of temperature and pressure, it can be a solid, liquid, or gas. Solid UF_6 is a white, dense, crystalline material that resembles rock salt. See http://web.evs .anl.gov/uranium/guide/uf6/index.cfm.

13. Global Security Newswire, "Israeli Raid Targeted Syrian Nuclear Reactor," 15 October 2007, http://www.nti.org/gsn/article/israeli-raid-targeted-syrian -nuclear-reactor/.

14. Mark Hibbs, "The Unspectacular Future of the IAEA Additional Protocol," *Proliferation Analysis*, 26 April 2012, http://carnegieendowment.org/2012 /04/26/unspectacular-future-of-iaea-additional-protocol/ahhz#.

15. Negative security assurances involve a pledge by NWSs not to use or threaten to use nuclear weapons against NNWSs. Positive security assurances mean a pledge to come to the aid of NNWSs that are nevertheless subject to a nuclear threat or attack.

16. Russia signed the "Memorandum on Security Assurances in Connection with Ukraine's Accession to the Treaty on the Non-Proliferation of Nuclear Weapons," http://unterm.un.org/DGAACS/unterm.nsf/WebView /4FE5EA3E98FBFF4E852569FA00008AAE?OpenDocument.

17. For instance, see James J. Wirtz, "Conclusions," in *Security Assurances and Nuclear Nonproliferation*, ed. Jeffrey W. Knopf (Stanford: Stanford University Press, 2012): 279–80.

18. For the details, see Pierre Goldschmidt, "Safeguards Noncompliance: A Challenge for the IAEA and the UN Security Council," *Arms Control Today* 40, no. 1 (January/February 2010), http://www.armscontrol.org/act /2010_01-02/Goldschmidt; and Pierre Goldschmidt, "Strengthening the Non-proliferation Regime," paper presented to the 7th ROK-UN Joint Conference on Disarmament and Non-proliferation Issues, Jeju Island, 24–26 November 2008, http://carnegieendowment.org/files/goldschmidt _rok_20081124.pdf.

19. Roehrig, "North Korea's Nuclear Weapons."

20. Tae-hong Kim, "South Korea Needs Precision Strike Capability," *Daily NK*, 15 September 2010. Quoted in Bruce E. Bechtol Jr., "Planning for the Unthinkable: Countering a North Korean Nuclear Attack and Management of Post-Attack Scenarios," *The Korean Journal of Defense Analysis* 23, no. 1 (March 2011), 9.

21. Ted Galen Carpenter, "Learn to live with a nuclear North Korea," *The Washington Post*, 14 February 2013, http://img.washingtonpost.com/opinions /learn-to-live-with-a-nuclear-north-korea/2013/02/14/0c6dad22-6fa9-11e2 -aa58-243de81040ba_story.html.

22. Victor Cha and Ellen Kim, "UN Security Council Passes New Resolution 2094 on North Korea," 7 March 2013. Center for Strategic and International Studies, http://csis.org/publication/un-security-council-passes-new -resolution-2094-north-korea. Another study argues that "China's trade with and investment in the North has mushroomed over the past ten years, rising from about $1 billion to over $6 billion—in an economy whose nominal GDP is just $28 billion." See William Tobey, "North Korea's Nuclear Test of China," Center for Strategic and International Studies (CSIS), 13 March 2013, http:// belfercenter.ksg.harvard.edu/files/NorthKoreaNuclearTestofChina.pdf.

23. Kelsey Davenport, "U.S. Seeking Unity for N. Korea Talks," *Arms Control Today* 43, no. 6 (July/August 2013), 39.

24. David Chance and Jack Kim, "North Korean Nuclear Test Draws Anger, Including from China," *Reuters*, 12 February 2013, http://www.reuters.com /article/2013/02/12/us-korea-north-idUSBRE91B04820130212.

25. Secretary of Defense Chuck Hagel, "Missile Defense Announcement," 15 March 2013, http://www.defense.gov/speeches/speech.aspx?speechid=1759.

26. To this author's understanding, it was not until the UN Economic Commission for Asia and Pacific (ECAFE) announced in 1968 the potential oil reserve under the seabed in the East China Sea that China began to claim its sovereignty over the Senkaku Islands.

27. See, for instance, Chen Qi, "Mitigating Tensions on the Korean Peninsula," Carnegie Endowment for International Peace, 10 April 2013, http://carnegietsinghua.org/2013/04/10/mitigating-tensions-on-korean-peninsula/fyzr.

28. In April 2013, a report by the US Defense Intelligence Agency (DIA) stated that the agency had "moderate confidence" that North Korea had mastered the ability to put a nuclear warhead on top of a ballistic missile. But the DIA assessment was denied by Secretary of State John Kerry and Director of National Intelligence James Clapper, saying North Korea has not "fully developed, tested or demonstrated the full-range of capabilities necessary for a nuclear-armed missile." See Rachel Oswald, "DOD Intel Views on N. Korea's Nuke Advances Not Shared by Other Agencies: Clapper," *Global Security Newswire*, 18 April 2013, http://www.nti.org/gsn/article/pentagon-intel-views-north-koreas-nuke-advances-not-shared-other-agencies-clapper/.

29. US Department of Defense, *Ballistic Missile Defense Review Report*, February 2010, p. 4, http://www.defense.gov/bmdr/docs/BMDR%20as%20of%2026JAN10%200630_for%20web.pdf. For the technical difficulties Pyongyang now faces in achieving a reliable long-range nuclear-armed ballistic missile, see Dana Struckman and Terence Roehrig, "Not So Fast: Pyongyang's Nuclear Weapons Ambitions," *Georgetown Journal of International Affairs*, 20 February 2013, http://journal.georgetown.edu/not-so-fast-pyongyangs-nuclear-weapons-ambitions-by-dana-struckman-and-terence-roehrig/.

30. Joel S. Wit and Jenny Town, "7 Reasons to Worry bout North Korea's Weapons," *The Atlantic*, 16 April 2013, http://www.theatlantic.com/international/archive/2013/04/7-reasons-to-worry-about-north-koreas-weapons/275020/.

31. Duyeon Kim, "Fact Sheet: North Korea's Nuclear and Ballistic Missile Programs," Center for Arms Control and Non-Proliferation, July 2013, http://armscontrolcenter.org/publications/factsheets/fact_sheet_north_korea_nuclear_and_missile_programs/.

32. Graham Allison, "The Specter of Nuclear Proliferation," *Los Angeles Times*, 17 February 2005, http://articles.latimes.com/2005/feb/17/opinion/oe-allison17.

CHAPTER 3

Humanitarian Implications of the North Korea Problem

Utpal VYAS

The implications of the continuing humanitarian crisis in North Korea are profound for states in the East Asia region.[1] The suffering of the people of North Korea should induce consideration on moral grounds alone, but apart from this there are also more direct strategic and long-term international political issues that affect all regional states, and need to be considered seriously.

According to recent UN estimates, out of a population of 25 million people, 16 million North Korean people's basic food security needs are not being met, and 2.8 million people require food aid on a regular basis in order to survive.[2] Despite aid being provided by the international community through the UN's World Food Program (WFP) and through NGOs, food crises recur on a regular basis. Among children under the age of five, 27.9 percent suffer from chronic malnutrition while 29 percent suffer from anemia. Meanwhile, the basic medical and educational infrastructure that might help alleviate problems is steadily deteriorating.

The primary causes of these problems include poor governance, a state ideology that prevents significant trade and communication with the outside world, and international sanctions linked to North Korea's nuclear weapons development. While other states in the region can do little in the face of the North Korea regime's continued hostile attitude and domestic repression,

attitudes toward humanitarianism in the region and the strategic implications of various options for humanitarian aid are important questions, which
in the long term may have a positive or negative impact on the lives of North
Korean people and their future relations with other citizens of East Asia.

This chapter considers regional attitudes to humanitarianism in general, then the regional response to humanitarian disaster in North Korea,
including the question of regional attitudes to the emerging "responsibility
to protect" (R2P) international doctrine. It will also consider the strategic
implications of continued humanitarian crises and how they affect relations
in the region. It will argue that international humanitarianism as a concept
is not well developed in the region, while in addition regional attitudes to
humanitarian crises in North Korea are hardening.

HUMANITARIAN PRINCIPLES

Humanitarianism is an idea with roots in liberalism and human rights thinking, based on the idea that all people have an equal right to life. Although
humanitarianism is usually ascribed to Western philosophical and religious
traditions,[3] international humanitarianism is implied in the UN Charter, as
well as various international conventions allowing for aid and relief in conflict
situations. The UN General Assembly in 1991 stipulated that humanitarian
relief should be provided impartially, neutrally, and with humanity, and in
2004 added the principle that relief should be separated from any political
or economic objectives of interested parties.[4]

Humanitarianism as a secular principle and general norm in international
politics has been developing through the twentieth century, along with
norms of human rights and international law, and the growth of modern
nongovernmental organizations (NGOs). In particular since the end of the
Cold War, there has been growth in humanitarian aid and intervention.[5] In
more recent years the doctrine of a state's "responsibility to protect" (R2P)
has been espoused by some NGOs and governments based on humanitarian
ideas. R2P will be discussed further in a later section. Firstly, it is necessary
to ask how humanitarianism as a principle is regarded in the East Asian
region. Is it based solely on Western notions of human rights, or is it a

principle that might be applied by governments and organizations in East Asia, in particular with regard to events in North Korea?

HUMANITARIANISM IN EAST ASIA

Humanitarianism implies a universal principle of protection of human rights regardless of national borders or citizenship. While democratization has proceeded in various parts of East Asia, the development of nation states and nationalism is still a very pressing concern for most governments in the region. Independence from colonial powers is still fresh in the collective memories of many peoples, and there are numerous cases where national borders and sovereignty are still contested by states, as well as by non-state actors and ethnic groups pushing for autonomy or independence. Hence it must be said that in general in East Asia, national sovereignty is emphasized more than any rights to interfere in neighboring countries' affairs. This has been clear from the ways in which ASEAN (the Association of Southeast Asian Nations) countries have proceeded with regional integration while tiptoeing around issues of sovereignty pooling,[6] as well as from numerous statements on intervention from officials from China and other East Asian states.

In connection with this, "developmental states"[7] in the region are focused on national economic development, which seems to preclude significant economic aid to other countries. To the extent that international transactions can promote national development, trade and investment is prioritized over international aid; this can be seen in the generally small amounts of humanitarian aid provided by governments in the region,[8] especially when compared with other financial and trade flows.

Developmental states in the region also tend to have strong, authoritarian central governments that can carry out industrial policies and development strategies. These kinds of regimes are also traditionally hostile to alternative centers of political power; therefore NGOs are not generally encouraged to develop to a large scale. However, democratization is proceeding in some East Asian countries, and NGO groups have also been developing along with the relaxation of central political control.[9] In particular in Japan,[10] but also in South Korea, Taiwan, Indonesia, and other countries, NGOs are slowly gaining strength. Illustrative of this is the response to the devastating Typhoon Haiyan that hit the Philippines in 2013. The largest state donations came from Western and Middle Eastern countries, with the only large aid package from an Asian nation coming from Japan. There is evidence, however, that many donations came from individuals, private organizations, and NGOs based in East Asia,[11] which demonstrates to some extent the spread of international humanitarian ideas in civil society in the region. Nevertheless, in relation to the state-provided humanitarian aid of Japan and other countries, private humanitarian aid in East Asia is disorganized and relatively small in scale.

HUMANITARIAN RESPONSES TO CRISIS IN NORTH KOREA

Attitudes to humanitarian crises in North Korea have been hardening, in the East Asia region as well as further abroad.[12] This may be partly due to the underlying attitudes toward humanitarianism described earlier; however it is also likely to be due to the continuing provocative actions and uncooperative behavior exhibited by the North Korea regime that have deterred other countries from providing any assistance. Pyongyang admitted to a uranium enrichment program in 2002, and in 2006 conducted its first nuclear test to wide international disquiet. Despite the continuation of the Six-Party Talks (6PT) forum set up to deal with North Korea's nuclear issues, a second nuclear test along with long-range missile tests were conducted by the regime in 2009; in both cases, food aid as well as other technical assistance were reduced sharply or stopped. Furthermore, according to its own ideological priorities, the regime at various times increases restrictions on the ability of foreign workers and NGOs to operate inside the country.[13] Finally, poor infrastructure and governance issues (corruption and political interference) lead to difficulties in actually ensuring food aid reaches those who need it.

Haggard et al. show the change in food import requirements and the amount of food actually made available in North Korea.[14] After the devastating 1995 famine throughout the country, a combination of international aid and improved domestic production reduced the difference between the population's food requirements and the amount of food available, until in 1999 the total demand for food was being met by domestic production, food aid, and imports. Since that time, due to a combination of mismanagement and reduction in food aid by the United States and South Korea in particular, the situation has been growing steadily worse again for North Korean people.

The UN estimated that in 2013 only 34.4 percent of the necessary food assistance had been received through the World Food Program. Furthermore, the United Nations Food and Agriculture Organization (UNFAO) estimated that only 5.4 percent of required funds had been obtained, while UNICEF estimated that only 7.4 percent of funding requirements had been met. In absolute terms, food aid in 2011 sank to almost zero.[15]

Haggard et al. suggest that there has been less food aid due to a relative improvement in food production in some years, or at least a perception among donors that this is the case.[16] There is also the increasing impression among food aid providers that food aid is not getting to the people who actually need it. Due to this, donors such as the United States have been providing a greater proportion of their aid through NGOs rather than through the North Korea regime, which cannot guarantee delivery. The United States decided to resume food aid to North Korea in 2008 in response to warnings of crisis from the UN, and following negotiations with North Korea at the Six-Party Talks; however in 2009 Pyongyang decided to refuse further aid and US NGO workers were told to leave the country. North Korea had reportedly disagreed with Washington on the number of foreign workers and Korean speakers allowed into the country,[17] and furthermore there were reports that the North Korea United Nations Development Programme (UNDP) offices were accused of mismanagement of funds and food aid.[18]

The perception among citizens of food aid donor countries also contributes to government policies. For example in Japan, where there is ample coverage of North Korea's nuclear and missile programs in the media, as well as the issue of abduction of Japanese citizens by the North Korea regime in the 1970s, opinion surveys indicate there is almost no awareness of humanitarian issues.[19] In China, North Korea's main source of aid and trade, the mainstream media characterize China–North Korea relations as being at their worst in years,[20] and China's government has begun to move against North Korea's financial operations in China.[21] Hence, there does not appear to be any public pressure to strengthen humanitarian assistance to North Korea in neighboring states; the opposite is more likely.

NON-STATE ACTORS

There is some evidence that the lack of progress on state-to-state aid, and the issues of mismanagement of funds, has led to governments supporting local NGOs' humanitarian activities. For example the European Union requires NGOs to have local offices (residence) if they are to receive funds, and this has led to several NGOs having a permanent presence in North Korea. US, South Korean, and Japanese NGOs tend to be nonresident with offices in South Korea or elsewhere, working through other contacts in North Korea, or among North Korean refugee communities in China and South Korea. South Korean NGO activities in North Korea have been restricted since 2007, after the election of the Grand National Party to the South Korean government.[22] The relative opening up of North Korea to foreign NGOs since the 1995 famine does seem to have contributed to the flow of information about the outside world into North Korea, as well as helping outsiders understand more about the North Korean population.[23]

However, if NGOs are not able to operate in the country, they are not able to perform their primary tasks, which are, in most cases at least, humanitarian. If the North Korea regime suspects even slightly that NGOs have political and ideological motives, it is unlikely to allow them to operate. Hence, it is arguable that humanitarian NGOs should emphasize their non-state nature, and completely refrain from activities which could provoke the regime if they actually want to help North Korean people. If NGOs have strategic aims, whether for their own members' interests or in collaboration with outside states, then they must expect to be blocked by the regime at some point. NGOs have tried a variety of strategies to balance their methods of operation, goals and ideological interests in such a way as to continue to operate in North Korea, with some cooperating with regime demands to use government distribution networks.[24]

Nevertheless, NGOs, as with any foreign operators, are subject to the survival calculations of the North Korea regime (i.e., suppression of any possible source of weakening of its ideological and political control of North Korean society). If the regime is determined to thwart the operations of a legitimate NGO, the NGO will be essentially powerless to carry out its aims.

RESPONSIBILITY TO PROTECT

How does the slowly developing doctrine of R2P affect the humanitarian situation in North Korea? R2P is based upon recommendations of the International Commission on Intervention and State Sovereignty (ICISS), an international body sponsored by the Canadian government and set up in response to a challenge from Kofi Annan, the Secretary General of the UN, in 1999.[25]

The ideas proposed were, based on the original UN Charter, that states have a responsibility to protect their citizens; rather than characterizing sovereignty as the right to control, it was to be reframed as a responsibility to protect. The ICISS report takes a broad view of this responsibility; sovereign states need to proactively protect their citizens from any threat to their welfare, to react to any crises, and to help rebuild after the events. This definition includes prevention of death by starvation[26] in addition to the prevention of genocide and death from natural disasters.

The doctrine of R2P was endorsed by the UN General Assembly in Resolution 60/1; however, this document primarily emphasizes the responsibility to protect against "genocide, war crimes, ethnic cleansing and crimes against humanity."[27] In other words, prevention of famine or starvation is not specifically considered. From subsequent discussions in the Security Council and General Assembly, there does not appear to be a willingness to intervene militarily to prevent starvation. Meanwhile, NGOs which campaign for the application of R2P focus on cases of state torture and violence against political prisoners as evidence against the North Korea regime,[28] perhaps because they know that this will more likely gain attention in the media and from governments than malnutrition and famine.

Despite the General Assembly's resolution, recent investigations by the Human Rights Council (UNHRC), which reports to the General Assembly, have included statements condemning the North Korea regime's use of starvation policies to maintain state control. The UNHRC's latest and most scathing report of February 2014 stated that North Korea has "used deliberate starvation as a means of control and punishment in detention facilities" and that "decisions, actions and omissions by the State and its leadership caused the death of at least hundreds of thousands of people and inflicted permanent physical and psychological injuries on those who survived."[29] Among the recommendations of the report are that the situation in North Korea be referred to the International Criminal Court (ICC) by the Security Council. However, the report does not directly mention R2P with regard to preventing famine and starvation.

Hence, there is no near- to medium-term likelihood that an intervention could occur in North Korea on the grounds that the regime was failing to protect its people from humanitarian disaster. Even in the marginally more likely case of an intervention on grounds of other crimes against humanity, in practice there is unlikely to be agreement in the Security Council on such a course of action due to suspicions of the intentions of Western intervention from China and Russia in particular. This is quite apart from the strategic calculations based on the high human and economic costs for any country that attempted to intervene militarily.

REGIONAL MULTILATERAL RESPONSES TO
HUMANITARIAN DISASTER IN NORTH KOREA

Multilateralism in East Asia is at an emergent stage. Trade and finance are the major multilateral concerns of countries in the region—the most advanced multilateral initiatives have been taken by Southeast Asian countries in the form of the ASEAN Free Trade Agreement, and by the wider region in the Chiang Mai Initiative Multilateral, a financial firefighting organization. In the realm of security, the ASEAN Regional Forum is the main meeting place for regional discussions, although it has not been able to initiate any specific agreements. More directly relevant to addressing the problems of North Korea, the Six-Party Talks (6PT) forum is the major regional multilateral initiative on North Korea, its members comprising South Korea, the United States, Russia, China, and Japan. The 6PT were set up to deal directly with issues of denuclearization in North Korea; as such the only assistance it has been prepared to offer is energy assistance in return for concrete steps to denuclearize by North Korea. In fact, a small amount of assistance has been given each time North Korea has decided to offer small steps toward halting its nuclear programs, with all 6PT members except for Japan having contributed at various stages.[30] Energy is indirectly important for humanitarian needs, as it is clearly required to operate agricultural and other industries as well as hospitals and other essential services. However, North Korea has restarted its nuclear and missile programs shortly after receiving aid in the past, and this has contributed to the reduction in energy assistance.

Meanwhile, regional coordination in providing food assistance has been almost nonexistent. The major multilateral organization that deals with delivering food aid to North Korea is the UN's World Food Program. Most food aid (over 90 percent[31]) delivered by the United States has been through this organ. However, the WFP, though multilateral, cannot be described as regional. The major regional concern of neighboring countries has been North Korea's nuclear program, and there is caution among regional states about linking humanitarian food aid to the issue of denuclearization, although in practice this does seem to have occurred, as is detailed further in the next section. Among the United States, South Korea, and Japan there is the possibility of more coordination on security regarding North Korea issues, but again there is no suggestion of coordination on humanitarian relief.

STRATEGIC CONSIDERATIONS AND HUMANITARIAN ASSISTANCE

While the ideal of humanitarian assistance has been to help people in distress regardless of ethnicity or nationality, the reality in a world of nation states and geopolitics has been that, particularly in the case of North Korea, humanitarian assistance is linked to strategic considerations. Thus, states that are interested in seeing North Korea stop and eventually eliminate its nuclear technology programs have explicitly or implicitly linked food and medical aid to progress on negotiations in this area, or have reduced or stopped humanitarian aid in response to nuclear tests, missile tests, and other belligerence from North Korea. For example in the case of the United States, which has been the largest donor of humanitarian assistance to North Korea, the debates and struggles of members of Congress over whether and how to link food assistance to foreign policy have been documented. While at some times the major concern about food aid has been the extent to which the United States can ensure through monitoring that the aid gets to people who actually need it, at other times food aid has been used in conjunction with negotiations over denuclearization.[32] China, which is normally North Korea's most reliable ally, is also suspected of using delays to its food and oil assistance to show displeasure over the regime's actions, especially in more recent years.[33] Meanwhile WFP data show that South Korea, since the election of the Grand National Party in 2007, has been among the strictest by applying a hardline policy that stops most food aid due to military and other provocations from the North.

North Korea's leadership also seems to use humanitarian assistance for its own purposes. The dilemma is how to keep enough food aid coming into the country to stave off economic and social collapse, while at the same time restricting the flow of information and political influence of outsiders, such as the WFP, foreign NGOs, and religious groups, in particular those from South Korea. Hence, in 2006 when Pyongyang tightened restrictions on foreign workers' movements, the WFP was forced to reduce its efforts to provide and distribute aid around the country.[34] In cases where foreign NGOs are allowed to move inside North Korea, they are always assigned government contacts that monitor or control their operations. Hence, it is clear that the regime's priorities lie in maintaining ideological control of its population rather than providing adequate sustenance to its citizens.

Therefore, in order to understand how to maintain humanitarian assistance to North Korean people, it may be necessary to model the calculations that the North Korean regime makes in order to ensure its own survival. The regime needs to obtain enough humanitarian assistance to stop its people from revolting against it, while at the same time keeping outside influence as low as possible in order to maintain its image as the only legitimate regime on the Peninsula and the image of North Korea's social system as the best system available to North Koreans. It also needs to ensure that most resources go to its supporters, while keeping less favored areas (often in the north of the country[35]) weak. Even when the regime desires some forms of economic development and international exchange, it needs to consider how to maintain this balance for its own survival. In fact, taking these calculations into account is, as Eberstadt has also argued, the only way in which humanitarian aid has been able to successfully help North Korean people in the past.[36]

FUTURE PROSPECTS

Considering the most recent evidence regarding North Korea's continued nuclear and missile development and reluctance to engage with the outside world except on its own terms, there is little prospect of regional neighbors or other countries responding in a significant way to humanitarian crises in North Korea. North Korea under Kim Jong Un is clearly following a familiar pattern of trying to ensure its own survival above all else in its own way. The only chance for citizens of North Korea to improve their human security is if the regime sees such a path as compatible with its own survival. In that sense, there is a chance that some economic reforms that allow for growth in North Korea's economy and stability for the regime may, as a side effect, improve the lives of North Korean citizens. In addition to this, if some openness to outside information is allowed as part of these reforms, there is a possibility that North Korean citizens will understand their collective problems more coherently, and demand reforms in some way.[37] There was some evidence of this happening after the currency reforms attempted by the regime in 2009, which led to reports of protests.[38] It is also becoming ever clearer that many North Korean citizens have access to outside information[39] in the form of pirated DVDs obtained from China or through the efforts of the United States and South Korea to broadcast information about the outside world into North Korea.

Apart from these potential domestic changes, there is a lack of any enthusiasm among regional neighbors to deal with a regime that is perceived to break commitments regularly. North Korea's only "ally," China, is the only likely source of longer-term economic assistance, and the increasing frustration among Chinese policymakers and advisors regarding North

Korea's nuclear program endangers that assistance. Nevertheless, North Korea–China trade seems to be booming,[40] and this increase in trade may be the only hope for North Korean citizens to improve their humanitarian situation in the short to medium term.

CONCLUSION

This chapter has given an overview of the humanitarian issues in North Korea and regional responses to it. It has pointed out that international humanitarianism is not a well-established concept in East Asia. The limited humanitarian aid that has been forthcoming from North Korea's regional neighbors is being reduced further as an indication of hardening attitudes toward North Korea generally, in particular due to its nuclear and missile programs, and its lack of good faith in implementing agreements. There is little public enthusiasm for humanitarian aid to North Korea; some donations are carried out by private citizens through NGOs, but due to media coverage, many people in East Asia are mainly concerned with North Korea's nuclear and missile programs. In any case, NGOs as well as international organizations such as the WFP find it increasingly difficult to operate in North Korea due to regime-imposed restrictions.

The emerging doctrine of responsibility to protect is unlikely to be applied in the case of North Korea, as the UN Security Council has not endorsed intervention to prevent famine, even if the famine is the result of state neglect and mismanagement, as is the case in North Korea. There has been some movement on the idea of holding North Korea responsible at the ICC for other human rights abuses such as state-sanctioned torture and other violence, but in practical terms international intervention to deal with such abuse is highly unlikely due to the probable high military and human costs.

Furthermore, regional multilateralism is still in its infancy in East Asia, as many states in the region are still grappling with their own internal developmental issues. Most regional multilateral efforts have gone into trade and finance (excluding North Korea), and there is no regional multilateral coordination on humanitarian assistance. The Six-Party Talks forum is the closest thing to regional coordination on North Korea issues, but humanitarian aid is not officially part of its agenda.

It is not impossible to envision some sort of regional coordination on humanitarian assistance; however it is likely that this would have some connection with strategic aspects of dealing with North Korea's denuclearization. If real coordination could be implemented, there would be a better chance of using policy carrots and sticks more effectively to actually ensure that humanitarian aid reaches the parts of the country and North Korean society where it is needed. In the absence of regime transformation or collapse, the best hope to improve the humanitarian situation in North Korea may be expanded trade and investment links with China in particular.

NOTES

1. For the purposes of this chapter, East Asia refers to Northeast as well as Southeast Asia.

2. UN, "Key Humanitarian Messages: Democratic People's Republic of Korea," 15 March 2013, accessed 19 August 2014, http://kp.one.un.org/content/uploads/2013/03/Key-Humanitarian-Messages-for-DPRK-15-March-2013.pdf.

3. Heiner Bielefeldt, "'Western' Versus 'Islamic' Human Rights Conceptions?: A Critique of Cultural Essentialism in the Discussion on Human Rights," *Political Theory* 28, no. 1 (2000).

4. UN Office for the Coordination of Humanitarian Affairs (OCHA), "OCHA on Message: Key Humanitarian Principles," OCHA, April 2010, accessed 19 August 2014, https://docs.unocha.org/sites/dms/Documents/OOM_HumPrinciple_English.pdf.

5. Michael N. Barnett, *The Empire of Humanity : A History of Humanitarianism* (Ithaca: Cornell University Press, 2011).

6. Utpal Vyas, "Regional Governance and Insitutions in Northeast Asia," in *Regional Indicators for Monitoring Regional Cooperation and Integration in East and Northeast Asia* (Bangkok: United Nations [forthcoming]).

7. Chalmers Johnson, *MITI and the Japanese Miracle: The Growth of Industrial Policy* (Stanford: Stanford University Press, 1982); Meredith Woo-Cumings, ed., *The Developmental State* (Ithaca: Cornell University Press, 1999).

8. Oliver Buston and Kerry Smith, *Global Humanitarian Assistance Report 2013* (Bristol: Development Initiatives, 2013).

9. Cain Nunns, "Asian NGOs, Awash with Cash, Ride a Wave of Economic Growth," *Guardian*, 26 July 2011, accessed 21 September 2014, http://www.theguardian.com/society/2011/jul/26/asian-ngos-tzu-chi-nunns.

10. Utpal Vyas, "Japan's International NGOs: A Small but Growing Presence in Japan-China Relations," *Japan Forum* 22, no. 3 (2010).

11. OCHA, "Typhoon Haiyan: Funding," March 2013, http://www.unocha.org /crisis/typhoonhaiyan/funding (accessed 19 August 2014).

12. Shaun Waterman, "China Stops Oil Exports to North Korea, Possibly as Punishment for Nuclear Test," *Washington Times*, 22 March 2013, accessed 21 September 2014, http://www.washingtontimes.com/news/2013/mar/22 /china-stops-oil-exports-north-korea-possibly-punis/.

13. Mark E. Manyin and Mary Beth D. Nikitin, "Foreign Assistance to North Korea," CRS Report R40095 (Washington, DC: United States Congressional Research Service, 2 April 2014), accessed 16 April 2014, http://www.fas.org/sgp/crs/row/R40095.pdf.

14. Stephan Haggard, Marcus Noland, and Erik Weeks, *North Korea on the Precipice of Famine* (Washington, DC: Peterson Institute for International Economics, May 2008), 20, accessed 20 August 2014, http://www.iie.com /publications/papers/noland0508.pdf.

15. WFP, "Food Aid Information System," accessed 19 August 2014, http:// www.wfp.org/fais/.

16. Haggard, Noland, and Weeks, *North Korea on the Precipice of Famine*.

17. Mark E. Manyin and Mary Beth D. Nikitin, "Foreign Assistance to North Korea" (Washington, DC: United States Congressional Research Service, 2 April 2014), 14, accessed 21 September 2014, http://www.refworld.org /docid/51d53c9f4.html.

18. Bay Fang, "Audit: Agencies in North Korea Broke UN Rules," *Chicago Tribune*, 8 June 2007, accessed 27 March 2014, http://articles.chicagotribune .com/2007-06-08/news/0706080233_1_north-korea-undp-currency.

19. Cabinet Office of Japan, "Gaiko ni Kan Suru Yoron Chosa - Kita Chosen e no Kanshin Jiko [Opinion Survey on Foreign Policy - Items of Interest Regarding North Korea]" (2010), accessed 21 September 2014 (no longer available), http://www8.cao.go.jp/survey/h25/h25-gaiko/zh/z23.html.

20. Celia Hatton, "Is China Ready to Abandon North Korea?," *BBC News*, 12 April 2013, accessed 21 September 2014, http://www.bbc.co.uk/news /world-asia-china-22062589.

21. Heng Xie and Megha Rajagopalan, "Bank of China Closes Account of Key North Korean Bank," *Reuters*, 7 May 2013, accessed 13 September 2014, http://www.reuters.com/article/2013/05/07/us-korea-north-china-bank -idUSBRE9460CX20130507.

22. Mi Ae Taylor and Mark E. Manyin, *Non-Governmental Organizations' Activities in North Korea*, CRS Report R41749 (Washington, DC: United

States Congressional Research Service, 25 March 2011), accessed 5 December 2013, http://fas.org/sgp/crs/row/R41749.pdf.

23. Edward P. Reed, "Unlikely Partners: Humanitarian Aid Agencies and North Korea," in *A New International Engagement Framework for North Korea?: Contending Perspectives*, eds. Ch'ung-yong An, Nick Eberstadt, and Yong-son Yi (Washington, DC: Korea Economic Insitute of America, 2004); Stephan Haggard and Marcus Noland, *Witness to Transformation: Refugee Insights into North Korea* (Washington, DC: Peterson Institute for International Economics, 2011); Hazel Smith, *Overcoming Humanitarian Dilemmas in the DPRK* (North Korea) (Washington, DC: United States Institute of Peace, July 2002), accessed 13 September 2014, http://www.usip.org/publications /overcoming-humanitarian-dilemmas-in-the-dprk-north-korea.

24. Taylor and Manyin, *Non-Governmental Organizations' Activities in North Korea*.

25. ICISS, "The Responsibility to Protect," International Commission on Intervention and State Sovereignty, Ottawa, December 2001, accessed 5 December 2013, http://idl-bnc.idrc.ca/dspace/bitstream/10625/18432/6 /IDL-18432.pdf.

26. Ibid., 33.

27. UN, "Resolution of the General Assembly 60/1 2005 World Summit Outcome," 2005, p. 30, accessed 29 March 2014, http://www.refworld.org /docid/44168a910.html.

28. Human Rights Watch, "North Korea: UN Should Act on Atrocities Report," 17 February 2014, accessed 2 September 2014, http://www.hrw.org/news /2014/02/17/north-korea-un-should-act-atrocities-report.

29. UNHRC, "Report of the Commission of Inquiry on Human Rights in the Democratic People's Republic of Korea," United Nations Human Rights Council, 7 February 2014, p. 11, accessed 25 September 2014, http://www.ohchr.org/EN/HRBodies/HRC/RegularSessions/Session25/ Documents/A-HRC-25-63_en.doc.

30. Manyin and Nikitin, "Foreign Assistance to North Korea," 6.

31. Ibid., 9.

32. Ibid., 12.

33. "Scale of Yearly Chinese Unconditional Aid to North Korea Revealed," *Dong-a Ilbo*, 24 June 2012, accessed 8 April 2014, http://english.donga.com /srv/service.php3?biid=2012062508548; Waterman, "China Stops Oil Exports to North Korea, Possibly as Punishment for Nuclear Test."

34. Manyin and Nikitin, *Foreign Assistance to North Korea*, 14.

35. Taylor and Manyin, *Non-Governmental Organizations' Activities in North Korea*.

36. Nicholas Eberstadt, *Western Aid: The Missing Link for North Korea's Economic Revival?* (Washington, DC: American Enterprise Institute, 26 April 2011), accessed 21 September 2014, http://papers.ssrn.com/sol3/papers.cfm?abstract_id=2022371.

37. Andrei Lankov, *The Real North Korea: Life and Politics in the Failed Stalinist Utopia* (New York: Oxford University Press, 2013), 215.

38. Sang-Hun Choe, "North Korea Revalues Its Currency," *New York Times*, 1 December 2009, accessed 17 September 2014, http://www.nytimes.com/2009/12/02/business/global/02korea.html.

39. Haggard and Noland, *Witness to Transformation*.

40. Aidan Foster-Carter, "South Korea Has Lost the North to China," *Financial Times*, 20 February 2014, accessed 17 September 2014, http://www.ft.com/intl/cms/s/0/f8fca490-9a23-11e3-a407-00144feab7de.html#axzz3Daza2LIl.

CHAPTER 4

Strategic Ramifications of the North Korea Nuclear Weapons Crisis

Denny ROY

Pyongyang clearly believes that deploying nuclear weapons enhances North Korea's security. That idea is debatable. What is more certain is that North Korea's deployment of nuclear weapons decreases security for the region as a whole, intensifying a host of strategic problems and dilemmas for the major Northeast Asian states. This chapter will evaluate these problems from the standpoint of the United States, China, South Korea, and Japan, explaining why they find it difficult to rally around a common policy solution.

NUCLEAR WEAPONS AND SECURITY

Nuclear weapons can theoretically introduce greater stability into an international subsystem (i.e., a group of states in the same geographic region) by making war less likely.[1] The strategic situation in Northeast Asia as described by Pyongyang's media and diplomats fits this scenario. The Democratic People's Republic of Korea (DPRK) argues that its nuclear weapons are necessary to deter alleged plans by the United States and South Korea to invade and overthrow the Kim regime, thereby substituting a cautious military stalemate where there would otherwise be aggression.[2] North Korean fears of attack are not unfounded. The country was heavily bombed during the Korean conflict of 1950–1953. US officials several times seriously considered using nuclear weapons against the DPRK.[3] By the 1990s, the dramatic disparity in wealth and economic power between North and South Korea, the DPRK's shortfalls in fuel supplies and training for its military units, and the natural disasters that caused malnutrition and even starvation in the North removed any doubt that South Korea's conventional military forces were superior to those of the DPRK (although Pyongyang's forces remained capable of causing terrible devastation in South Korea's capital city of Seoul).

Today, in terms of the basic sources of national strategic strength, North Korea is at a massive disadvantage relative to South Korea. The Republic of Korea's (ROK) population is double the size of the DPRK's and much healthier, with South Koreans enjoying a longer average life expectancy by ten years. The DPRK has a disproportionately large military, but the ROK's is better trained and equipped. Although North Korea under the Songun ("military first") policy spends a whopping 22 percent of its GDP on its armed forces and the ROK less than 3 percent, South Korean spending still dwarfs North Korea's, $26 billion to $8 billion. The ROK's economy overall is forty times the size of the DPRK's and is also much more technologically advanced.[4] A final reason for Pyongyang to feel insecure is that North Korea was one of the three states President George W. Bush called out in 2002 as part of an "axis of evil" before the United States led an invasion of one of the three, Iraq, the following year.

Nevertheless, the argument that North Korea needs nuclear weapons for its own self-defense, and that a DPRK nuclear capability makes the region less war-prone, is questionable on several grounds. If the United States and the ROK planned to invade North Korea and overthrow its regime, they had ample opportunity before the DPRK demonstrated a nuclear capability. The DPRK's first nuclear explosion in 2006 indicated the beginning of a limited time window before North Korea would have a deliverable nuclear weapon, a capability that would greatly raise the potential costs to an adversary planning to go to war against the DPRK. Eight years on, the orientation of Seoul and Washington toward Pyongyang remains defensive, not offensive. One important reason is that South Koreans, especially younger generations, are in no hurry to take on the economic burden of absorbing the poor country to their north.[5]

Nuclear weapons apparently have a domestic political purpose for the DPRK regime beyond the strategic purpose. The nuclear program substantiates the regime's domestic political argument that North Korea is poor not because the regime is incompetent, but because powerful outside enemies are trying to destroy the country. Bringing North Korea into the exclusive and prestigious nuclear club was perhaps the most politically significant legacy of Kim Jong Il, who presided over an otherwise dismal period of DPRK history that saw the government fail to deliver on its promises of prosperity for the North Korean populace. The prestige of Kim Il Sung and Kim Jong Il are the basis of the current regime's legitimacy.

North Korea's policy of intentionally raising tensions with over-the-top belligerent rhetoric and occasional lethal provocations indicates that Pyongyang is not fearful of an imminent US or ROK attack, but rather is confident enough to use threats and intimidation as a strategy for gaining concessions from its adversaries. Pyongyang, for example, rushed to threaten the US homeland with a nuclear strike as early as March 2013, long before demonstrating the capability to deliver a nuclear weapon over such a distance. Demonstrating a willingness to fight if attacked is consistent with a strategy that prioritizes deterrence. North Korea's belligerent posture, however, goes so far beyond this standard as to force the South Koreans and their US allies to consider a policy of regime overthrow for *their own* defense. In other words, the nuclear program is at least as much an offensive diplomatic weapon for Pyongyang as a defensive military weapon. It is the basis for the Kim regime's demand that Washington begin treating Pyongyang as an equal.

Finally, it is worth noting that China, which is sympathetic to the North's sense of insecurity, takes the position that Pyongyang should denuclearize.[6]

THE UNITED STATES

The principal pillar of US influence in the Western Pacific is the country's ability to protect its allies and friends. Close allies South Korea and Japan are the countries most gravely endangered by the DPRK's nuclear weapons program—not only because of their relative proximity to the DPRK, but also because of Pyongyang's hostility toward them. South Korea, disparaged as a "puppet" of Washington, is Pyongyang's rival for rule over the Peninsula. Japan is deeply vilified for its occupation of Korea in the twentieth century. A deliverable nuclear weapon would give Pyongyang an offensive capability that neither Japan nor the ROK could directly counter by themselves because neither has its own nuclear weapons. Japan has a ballistic missile defense system and Seoul is building one, but the efficacy of such systems is unproven. Pyongyang has already made thinly veiled nuclear threats against both the ROK and Japan.[7] There are at least three possible negative consequences from the United States' standpoint. First, through implied or explicit nuclear blackmail, Pyongyang might intimidate Seoul or Japan into breaking ranks from preferred US policies. Second, the fear of Pyongyang's nuclear capability might cause one or both of the US allies to lose confidence in the US "nuclear umbrella," or the US commitment to retaliate against a nuclear attack upon them as if it was an attack against the United States. Third, Seoul and Tokyo might decide to deploy their own nuclear arsenals, in contravention of Washington's interest in preventing further nuclear proliferation.

The DPRK's nuclear weapons program also poses two distinct threats to the US homeland. The first is the possibility of North Korea launching a nuclear-armed missile at a US city. As of this writing, the DPRK appears to have neither a reliable long-range intercontinental missile that could accomplish this task nor a sufficiently miniaturized nuclear explosive that such a missile could carry. Clearly, however, North Korea is working on both capabilities and is likely to succeed within a few years. The rocket launches the DPRK periodically carries out as part of its "space program" are essentially test firings of unarmed intercontinental ballistic missiles (ICBMs). The test in December 2012 showed significant progress over previous failures. Pyongyang claimed its February 2013 nuclear test involved a "miniaturized" bomb, and the US Department of Defense said in 2013 the DPRK might have already built a bomb small enough to mount on a missile.[8]

The likelihood that Pyongyang would actually launch a nuclear attack against the United States is nearly zero because the US retaliatory second-strike would virtually assure the destruction of the North Korean regime and state. Nevertheless, if and when that day arrives, the reaction of the

United States to the news that it is within range of North Korea's nuclear missiles is likely to be one of extreme alarm. This is because over many years the US media have consistently described North Korea's government as irrational (usually using terms such as "unpredictable" or "erratic") and hyperbelligerent. To be sure, Pyongyang has largely and perhaps intentionally contributed to its image in the United States as a crazy and risk-acceptant state. The problem is that the combination of North Korea's capability and already-expressed intent will cause the US public to demand a response by Washington to ensure continued US security. The response might be disproportionate to the actual threat. Unless they are highly confident in their ballistic missile defense system, Americans might demand stronger consideration of a more active policy of promoting overthrow of the North Korean regime.

A more realistic threat posed by Pyongyang to the United States is proliferation of nuclear technology or fissile material to a third party, perhaps to a non-state terrorist group that has hostile intentions toward the United States. This is plausible because North Korea needs cash and has few scruples about how to raise it (Pyongyang has, for example, reportedly ordered its diplomats to smuggle illegal drugs to raise revenue[9]) and because DPRK leaders might believe they would not be implicated in a nuclear attack carried out by a non-DPRK group even if North Korea supplied the attackers. Thus, Pyongyang might determine it could score a lucrative deal and indirectly strike a staggering blow against its adversary without suffering a US retaliatory attack. Pyongyang's willingness to test the United States' fortitude on this point cannot be casually dismissed. North Korea helped Syrians build a plutonium-based nuclear program, along the lines of the plant in Yongbyon, until an Israeli air strike knocked it out in 2007.[10] For these reasons dismantling the nuclear weapons program is the top priority of US policy toward North Korea.

CHINA

China has a long-term strategic goal of avoiding military encirclement by countries that fear China's rise. An important element of China's campaign to avoid encirclement is to portray itself as a good international citizen that will uphold the current international system of laws, institutions, and norms rather than try to overthrow and replace it with a more self-serving regional order. Beijing thus insists that its foreign policy is consistently principled and responsible. To the extent, however, that Beijing shelters Pyongyang from the international consequences of the DPRK's outlaw behavior, China undercuts its own strategy. The DPRK nuclear weapons program has damaged China's international reputation as Beijing has sought to water down proposed sanctions against Pyongyang and counteracted these sanctions by continuing to trade heavily with North Korea.

Nuclear proliferation by North Korea strengthens the arguments for South Korea and Japan to develop their own nuclear arsenals. Either of these countries going nuclear—especially Japan—would be a major strategic setback from China's standpoint.

The nuclear weapons crisis worsens Sino-US relations. Superficially, denuclearization of North Korea appears to be a point of agreement and a basis for cooperation between Beijing and Washington. But in fact it is an additional strategic dispute that drives the two countries apart. While China supports denuclearization, this objective is second to stability—i.e., no change in the North Korean regime—because the Chinese fear the consequences of a collapse of the regime more than they fear the consequences of a nuclear-armed DPRK. China is unwilling to put strong pressure on Pyongyang to denuclearize because this might contribute to regime collapse. For the United States, these priorities are reversed: denuclearization is paramount, even at the risk of regime collapse, which Americans would generally welcome.

The result has been mutual frustration and increased suspicion between China and the United States. Many US observers assume China could force a shutdown of the DPRK nuclear program at will by cutting off transfers of food and energy, of which it is a major supplier to North Korea. That China has not done so despite professing a commitment to denuclearization convinces some US observers that Beijing is playing a double game.[11] China, on the other hand, insists that the United States overestimates Chinese influence, under-appreciates the dangers of regime collapse, and fails to understand that if the Chinese push too hard they will lose all of their influence as North Korea's leaders stop listening altogether.[12] A divided Korean Peninsula is in some ways strategically advantageous for

China. North Korea acts as a buffer state that keeps US ally South Korea and its US military bases at a distance from China's border. A united Korea would be a medium-sized power that might take a stronger position on the question of disputed territory just north of the China-DPRK border. If the northern part of the Korean Peninsula became prosperous under the administration of Seoul, Beijing's management of its large ethnic Korean population in the Manchurian provinces might become more problematic. Korean reunification might also threaten the deals China now has with the DPRK to extract North Korea's resources.

A stable, peaceful two-Korea scenario is therefore the ideal situation from China's standpoint. Unfortunately for Beijing, a divided Peninsula has proved *un*stable. Pyongyang's brinksmanship risks triggering a war on China's doorstep. War itself would be catastrophic for China. Conflict would at minimum disrupt at least some of the trade flows in the region, potentially causing an interruption in China's economic growth. A Korean war would almost certainly see South Korean and US forces crossing into northern Korea and heading in the direction of the Chinese frontier. A likely consequence of war would be the removal of the Pyongyang government, creating several potential problems for China including large numbers of North Korean refugees, banditry by renegade groups of former soldiers, and the expectation that China would help pay the costs of relief and reconstruction in the former DPRK.

Chinese leaders have urged North Korea to reform along the lines of the post-Mao Chinese model, with greater marketization of the economy and openness to trade with the outside world while maintaining an authoritarian political system and one-party rule. Pyongyang's nuclear weapons program, however, is part of an overall approach that rejects the Chinese model in favor of a bunker mentality that prioritizes military readiness over prosperity (the Songun policy).

SOUTH KOREA

The North Korea nuclear program poses a direct and existential threat to the ROK, substantiating past North Korea's threats to turn Seoul into a "sea of fire."[13] As with the United States, the danger of South Korea being victimized by an unprovoked DPRK nuclear attack is miniscule. Nuclear weapons make no sense as an offensive DPRK weapon against South Korea, as the North Koreans would be irradiating territory they hope to occupy. The danger, rather, is that DPRK nuclear weapons make inter-Korea relations more conflict-prone. This could happen in two ways. First, Pyongyang might overuse its nuclear capability in attempts to blackmail the South, causing the South Koreans to believe their security is so imperiled that they must attempt to destroy the DPRK's nuclear capability or perhaps even the regime itself through a conventional military attack.

The second way the North Korea nuclear program heightens tensions involves its impact on a potential conventional military exchange. In the decades following the Korean War, Pyongyang carried out several lethal attacks against South Korean citizens that could be considered acts of war. These included attacks against South Korean government leaders as well as civilians. In each of these instances it was clear that the attack was strictly limited in aim and scope, not the opening shot of a general war in which the North would send forces to attempt to overrun the South and replace its government. Consequently, Seoul did not retaliate militarily against these attacks. This seemingly solidified an expectation in Pyongyang that Seoul would not respond in kind to limited, isolated violence. The two attacks by the DPRK in 2010, however, generated a sea-change in ROK attitudes. An international investigation attributed the sinking of the South Korean corvette *Cheonan* in March, with the loss of forty-six ROK sailors, to a stealthy North Korean torpedo attack.[14] In November, North Korean artillery fire striking the island of Yeonpyeong killed four South Koreans. Previously, ROK public opinion had opposed retaliation in such situations, but after these attacks Seoul, with the support of a majority of South Koreans, publicly committed to carrying out a disproportionate military counter-strike if the DPRK should attack again. ROK President Park Geun-hye recently said, "It is important that there should be stern punishment for reckless provocations so as to break the vicious cycle that has been repeating."[15]

The post-2010 security situation is thus extraordinarily dangerous. Pyongyang, with few other cards to play, had established a pattern that included regular provocations, some of them lethal. Provocations became regular because Seoul's non-response meant Pyongyang did not pay a tangible price for the attacks except for foreign condemnation and in some cases additional economic sanctions. Sanctions have had little deterrent effect because the DPRK already had minimal economic interaction with the countries most interested in enforcing the sanctions (i.e., excluding China). Seoul attempted to break the pattern of provocations by promising that future lethal attacks would generate unprecedented ROK military retaliation against the DPRK. Such a scenario would pull both countries into uncharted waters, with obvious dangers of further escalation.

Nevertheless, whether DPRK leaders take Seoul's threat seriously is questionable. It is here that the DPRK's new nuclear capability makes a potentially crucial difference in the leadership's calculations. It is reasonable to postulate that at least some DPRK planners expect their nuclear capability will deter the ROK from launching a retaliatory military strike after a limited DPRK attack, out of fear that the third round would be a DPRK use of a nuclear weapon against the South. DPRK statements about the nuclear capability suggest this is precisely the idea Pyongyang is trying to plant in South Korean hearts.[16]

Thus the deterrent value of Seoul's tougher new stance may in practice be negated by the North's nuclear program. Although the danger that Pyongyang would actually use nuclear weapons on the southern part of the Korean Peninsula cannot be discounted, the greater danger of the DPRK's nuclear weapons program is that it potentially emboldens North Korea to make the first-round conventional attack that Seoul might have otherwise successfully deterred. Given the likelihood of a disproportionately strong South Korean counterattack, it is not difficult to imagine North Korean strategists arguing to the paramount leader that a third-round response by the DPRK is necessary to avoid Seoul drawing the conclusion that South Korea could now attack North Korea at will without a response, a situation that would create a state of permanently increased vulnerability for the DPRK. After three rounds of attacks, each perhaps more destructive than the previous round, halting the continued escalation into general war would be a Herculean diplomatic task.

1950 REDUX?

Either war or regime collapse could draw US or South Korean troops across the 38th parallel into northern Korea. In the former case, intervention would be necessary to put down North Korean military resistance and to disarm DPRK troops. With the evaporation of DPRK governance and authority, troops from the alliance would be needed to restore order and to address the likely humanitarian crisis among the civilian population as well. Seoul would have strong incentives to quickly establish structures and processes to begin preparing the North for rule by the Republic of Korea government.

China, on the other hand, would have its own set of incentives not only to mitigate the possible chaos that might spread from northern Korea into China, but also to protect Chinese economic operations and interests and to keep US troops and influence as far as possible from China's border.

This could create a scenario in which alliance forces heading north meet China's forces heading south, with each side highly suspicious of the other's motives and both sides grasping the opportunity to reshape the status quo. It was a similar situation that led to fighting between the United States' and China's forces in Korea in 1950, a war neither side wanted or benefitted from. A Chinese general warned that without "consultation" of China, the intervention of US and South Korean troops would lead to "1950 all over again."[17] US government officials have privately reported that they frequently raise this issue, but their Chinese counterparts are unwilling to discuss it. It is understandable that China would worry about the impact such a discussion would have on relations with Pyongyang should the North Koreans become aware through the Americans revealing this secret either intentionally or unintentionally.

The DPRK nuclear weapons program intensifies this problem. It creates additional pressure for US military forces to rush into northern Korea in either a post-collapse or a general war scenario, as the US government will be anxious to gain control and possession over DPRK nuclear weapons, materials, and facilities as quickly as possible to avoid leakage into the international black market leading to further proliferation or nuclear terrorism. Washington may also wish to prevent South Korea coming under the temptation to achieve nuclear status by capturing the DPRK's program and arsenal. China would have a similar desire to re-establish control over DPRK nuclear sites and to prevent proliferation to South Korea. Nuclear weapons in the North increase the incentive for both sides to intervene with troops on the ground and the need for doing it quickly, thereby cutting down the time for ad hoc communication and coordination before Chinese and alliance personnel are in close proximity.

Former US Assistant Secretary of State Kurt Campbell said US and Chinese officials held secret talks on North Korea contingencies prior to the death of Kim Jong Il.[18] That report is encouraging, but the problem seems far from solved. Discussion does not necessarily mean agreement. The two sides may have gone no further than warning each other not to do what each is nevertheless committed to do. There are presently no public indications that such consultation has continued into the Kim Jong Un era, or if so whether these consultations have been deep and thorough enough to avoid unintended US-China conflicts in a collapse scenario.

JAPAN

Japan is under a direct threat from North Korea, a threat immeasurably intensified by the DPRK's nuclear weapons program. Pyongyang has frequently threatened military strikes against Japan, often in the midst of periods of high tension between Pyongyang and Seoul or Pyongyang and Washington, in which Tokyo had little or no involvement. During the crisis sparked by joint US-ROK military exercises in early 2012, for example, North Korean media warned that "the spark of war will touch Japan first" and said Tokyo would be "consumed in nuclear flames" if Japan tried to shoot down a DPRK missile.[19] Japan joins the ROK and the United States as countries against which Pyongyang has already threatened to use its nuclear weapons. As a country that lacks its own nuclear retaliatory capability and is outside of Korea's historical territory, Japan arguably has greater reason to fear a North Korean nuclear ICBM than the United States or South Korea. Because of its proximity to North Korea, Japan is within range of even the medium-range Nodong missile in addition to the long-range Musudan and Taepodong missiles. The North Korea missile threat has been a major security issue for Japan since 1998, when a DPRK test sent a missile into Japan's airspace. DPRK missiles are the ostensible motivation for Japan's heavy investment in defenses against ballistic missiles.

While Japan is under direct threat from the DPRK nuclear program, it has limited direct influence over North Korea. An accumulation of sanctions has left Japan with little economic interaction with the DPRK. The last significant lever disappeared when Tokyo tightened restrictions on the remittances of cash from Japan to North Korea in 2009. Tokyo has cut most of its communication channels to North Korea over the latter's nuclear tests. In 2002 Japanese Prime Minister Junichiro Koizumi and North Korea leader Kim Jong Il agreed that both countries would move toward normalization, but this agreement quickly foundered over Japan's demands regarding the abduction issue and the DPRK's pursuit of nuclear weapons. Prime Minister Shinzo Abe recently reiterated his willingness to meet with Kim Jong Un if Pyongyang handles the abductee problem to Tokyo's satisfaction. It is difficult, however, to foresee the two sides bridging that issue. Japanese public opinion ensures that the bar remains high, while North Korea's government insists that some of the abductees whose return Japan demands have died or were never in DPRK hands.

US policy toward North Korea has often not addressed Japan's security concerns. While Washington's top priority has been denuclearization, Tokyo is more concerned with the DPRK missile program. In 1993–1994 Japan's government worried that US-DPRK tensions would lead to a war that could affect Japan. Later Tokyo felt marginalized by Four-Party Talks that did not include a Japanese delegation. In 1998–2000 Tokyo was disappointed by a US response to the DPRK Taepodong missile launch that the Japanese believed was not tough enough. In 2002–2003 it was the opposite problem: Koizumi practiced summitry with Kim Jong Il while Washington demonized North Korea as part of the "axis of evil." Then in mid-decade Washington shut Tokyo out again as it pursued bilateral negotiations with the DPRK.[20]

Poor relations between Seoul and Tokyo due to historical legacy issues (disputed ownership of the Dokdo/Takeshima Islands, Yasukuni Shrine visits by Japanese leaders, the "comfort women," etc.) have prevented stronger cooperation against the common North Korea threat. A proposed bilateral agreement on military information sharing died amid public anti-Japan outcry in South Korea in 2012.

The security threat from North Korea, combined with responses from South Korea and the United States that from Japan's point of view are often less than ideal, has been one of the forces pushing Japan to gradually distance itself from the postwar restrictions on Japan's military capabilities and policy. One clear and tangible outcome has been the Abe government's interest in clearing the way for Japan to shoot down a North Korean missile heading toward US territory. In the eyes of China and South Korea, this movement toward "normalization" by Japan is a deterioration of regional security.

DIVIDED WE FAIL

A preventive war by the US-ROK alliance certainly merits serious consideration, both because of the military threat posed by Pyongyang and because of the internationally endorsed principle of "responsibility to protect" that is raised by the regime's poor treatment of its populace, intentionally through the imprisonment of tens of thousands for political offenses and unintentionally through economic mismanagement that has led to large-scale starvation and malnutrition. That option, however, is ruled out absent a first strike by Pyongyang. Even during the first North Korea nuclear weapons crisis of 1994, Washington balked at the idea of a precision strike aimed at destroying the DPRK's key nuclear facilities.[21] That was prior to the DPRK demonstrating a weapons capability, at a time when destroying a key, vulnerable piece of infrastructure might be expected to halt the program. The task would be much harder today without invasion and occupation because the arsenal can be easily dispersed and concealed. An even bigger reason why a cold military attack by the alliance is off the table is the fear that Seoul would be smashed amid the DPRK's death throes.

A less drastic option would be laying siege to North Korea until the regime agrees to give up its nuclear program. This option offers the prospect of changing the status quo without necessarily starting a war, although it does not guarantee no war, as Pyongyang might choose to carry out limited but escalating strikes in an attempt to intimidate its adversaries into lifting the siege. China would be the key component in such a strategy. As the major foreign supplier of North Korea's energy and food, China could by itself carry out a crushingly painful siege. Conversely, lack of participation by China would mostly negate the effect even of a vigorous cutoff of engagement with North Korea by the rest of the international community—although blocking the DPRK from using the international financial system would cause Pyongyang serious hardship. In any case, however, as long as China fears North Korean regime collapse more than North Korean nuclear weapons, the siege scenario remains a fantasy.

US policy toward North Korea has failed to prevent Pyongyang from building a workable bomb and is failing to prevent Pyongyang from making progress toward deploying a reliable and accurate nuclear-armed ICBM. Washington's policy for the last decade has been to insist on at least initial steps toward denuclearization by Pyongyang before any upgrade of the bilateral relationship can occur. Such an upgrade would start from a baseline of near zero, since the US has an economic embargo against North Korea and the two countries have no formal diplomatic relations with each other. South Korea's governments under Lee Myung Bak and Park Geun-hye have taken a similar line, although the DPRK tries to sideline Seoul and deal directly with the United States. Both the United States and the ROK have reaffirmed that North Korea could expect that the benefits of détente would more than compensate for whatever was lost through denuclearization. Pyongyang's response has been to insist that the DPRK will never consider giving up its nuclear weapons unless the United States denuclearizes first.[22]

Both the United States' and South Korea's governments have maintained the awkward stance of "not accepting" the DPRK as a nuclear weapons state while acknowledging that the DPRK has successfully exploded a nuclear bomb. As of early 2014, the argument that Washington and Seoul should compromise and strive to cap rather than eliminate the DPRK's nuclear and ballistic missile programs has not won over policymakers. Relations between North Korea and its adversaries therefore remain in a stalemate, awaiting some form of shock to the status quo.

Pyongyang's nuclear weapons program likely increases the danger that Pyongyang's brinksmanship could lead to war, which would be a disastrous outcome for each of the major players. With what they believe is a nuclear deterrent against US or South Korean attack, North Korea's leaders may feel emboldened to make more bellicose threats or to continue carrying out lethal provocations against South Korea. This in itself could easily escalate to general war. Furthermore, there is a serious risk of miscalculation as the

Pyongyang regime underappreciates that its nuclear weapons program represents a permanently increased level of threat to DPRK adversaries and thereby increases the costs to them of allowing North Korea's government to persist.

This is, unfortunately, a regional problem that defies a regional solution. None of the individual policies of the major Northeast Asian countries has by itself been effective in preventing nuclear proliferation in North Korea or in persuading Pyongyang to dismantle its program. The Northeast Asian states are similar in seeing the DPRK's nuclear weapons program as a strategic problem. They are dissimilar, however, in their approaches to dealing with that problem. Each of them prefers to live with the problem rather than adopt an approach that might bring about denuclearization, but at the cost of cutting against other important national interests.

NOTES

1. Kenneth Waltz, "The Spread of Nuclear Weapons: More May Be Better," *Adelphi Papers*, Number 171 (London: International Institute for Strategic Studies, 1981).

2. See, for example, Ri Hyo'n-to, "There Is No One Who Can Block Our People's Forward March Toward the Military-First Road," *Rodong Sinmun Online*, 18 August 2014, Open Source Center document KPR2014081808836627.

3. Marilyn B. Young, "Bombing Civilians: An American Tradition," *History News Network*, April 2009, accessed 10 January 2014, http://hnn.us/article/67717.

4. CIA World Factbook, accessed 31 January 2014, https://www.cia.gov/library/publications/the-world-factbook/; "South v North Korea: How Do the Two Countries Compare? Visualised," *Guardian*, 8 April 2013, accessed 31 January 2014, http://www.theguardian.com/world/datablog/2013/apr/08/south-korea-v-north-korea-compared.

5. Guy Taylor, "Young South Koreans Fear Unification with North Would Create Economic Burden," *Washington Times*, 10 April 2013, accessed 10 January 2014, http://www.washingtontimes.com/news/2013/apr/10/young-south-koreans-fear-unification-with-north-wo/?page=all.

6. "Xi-Obama Summit: US and China Agree North Korea Must Give Up Nuclear Weapons," Reuters News Service, 9 June 2013, accessed 11 September 2014, http://www.telegraph.co.uk/news/worldnews /northamerica/usa/10108442/Xi-Obama-summit-US-and-China-agree -North-Korea-must-give-up-nuclear-weapons.html.

7. "Japan Increasingly Nervous about North Korea Nuclear Threats," Associated Press, 8 April 2013, accessed 5 February 2014, http://www.foxnews.com /world/2013/04/08/us-may-be-out-nuclear-north-korea-reach-but-japan -fears-tokyo-us-bases-arent/.

8. Ernesto Londono, "Pentagon: North Korea Likely Has Capacity to Make Nuclear Warhead for Ballistic Missile," *Washington Post*, 11 April 2013, accessed 15 January 2014, http://www.washingtonpost.com/world/national -security/pentagon-north-korea-could-have-nuclear-missile/2013/04/11 /72230dea-a2eb-11e2-82bc-511538ae90a4_story.html.

9. "N. Korean Diplomats 'Sell Millions of Dollars Worth of Drugs,'" *Chosun Ilbo*, 20 March 2013, accessed 18 January 2014, http://english.chosun.com /site/data/html_dir/2013/03/20/2013032001084.html.

10. Dennis P. Halpin, "Syria and North Korea: A Real Axis of Evil," *National Interest*, 4 September 2013, accessed 5 February 2014, http://nationalinterest .org/commentary/syria-north-korea-real-axis-evil-8994.

11. Anne Applebaum, "The North Korean Threat That China Fosters," *Washington Post*, 2 June 2009, accessed 5 February 2014, http://www.washingtonpost.com /wp-dyn/content/article/2009/06/01/AR2009060102480.html.

12. Victor Cha, "Why China Cannot Cut Off North Korea," *Huffington Post*, 6 April 2012, accessed 5 February 2014, http://www.huffingtonpost.com /victor-cha/china-north-korea-relations_b_1404178.html.

13. "North Korea Threatens 'a Sea of Fire' upon South Korea," CNN, 25 November 2011, accessed 5 February 2014, http://www.cnn.com/2011/11/24 /world/asia/north-korea-sea-of-fire/.

14. Namgung Min, "Results Confirm North Korea Sank Cheonan," *Daily NK*, 20 May 2010, accessed 11 September 2014, http://www.dailynk.com/english /read.php?cataId=nk00100&num=6392.

15. "Park Calls for 'Stern Punishment' for N. Korean Provocations," *Yonhap News Service*, 22 February 2013, accessed 31 January 2014, http://english .yonhapnews.co.kr/national/2013/02/22/37/0301000000AEN2013022200 4951315F.HTML.

16. James Silcocks, "North Korea Threatens 'All-Out War, a Nuclear War' As It Announces It Is 'On War Footing' with South," *Independent*, 30 March 2013, accessed 5 February 2014, http://www.independent.co.uk/news/world/asia

/north-korea-threatens-allout-war-a-nuclear-war-as-it-announces-it-is-on
-war-footing-with-south-8554932.html.

17. Larry M. Wortzel, "PLA 'Joint' Operational Contingencies in South Asia,
Central Asia, and Korea," in B*eyond the Strait: PLA Missions Other than
Taiwan*, eds. Roy Kamphausen, David Lai, and Andrew Scobell (Carlisle,
PA: Strategic Studies Institute, US Army War College, April 2009), 346.

18. Shirley A. Kan, *China and Proliferation of Weapons of Mass Destruction and
Missiles: Policy Issues*, CRS Report RL31555 (Washington, DC: United
States Congressional Research Service, 3 January 2014), 24.

19. "John Kerry Hits Out as North Korea Threatens Japan," *news.com.au*,
12 April 2013, accessed 31 January 2014, http://www.news.com.au/world
/president-obama-says-the-united-states-will-take-all-necessary-steps-to
-protect-its-interests/story-fndir2ev-1226618722806.

20. Sheila A. Smith, "North Korea in Japan's Strategic Thinking," *Asan Forum*,
7 October 2013, accessed 31 January 2014, http://www.theasanforum.org
/north-korea-in-japans-strategic-thinking/#1.

21. Jamie McIntyre, "Washington Was on Brink of War with North Korea 5
Years Ago," CNN, 4 October 1999, accessed 5 February 2014, http://www
.cnn.com/US/9910/04/korea.brink/.

22. "DPRK's Nuclear Force Is Treasured Sword for Defending Nation: Rodong
Sinmun," Korean Central News Agency, 3 December 2013, accessed 5
February 2014, http://www.kcna.co.jp/item/2013/201312
/news03/20131203-09ee.html.

CHAPTER 5

Economic Engagement with North Korea

Yoshinori KASEDA

The implementation of the agreements reached in the Six-Party Talks (6PT) in February and October 2007 came to a halt in late 2008 due to confrontation between North Korea (DPRK) on one part and the United States, Japan, and South Korea (ROK) on the other over the verification of the North's detailed declaration of its nuclear program. Since then, the North Korea nuclear issue has become even more difficult to resolve because of North Korea's development of a uranium enrichment capability and its second and third nuclear tests in May 2009 and February 2013. The United Nations Security Council (UNSC) has strengthened economic sanctions against North Korea in response to the repeated nuclear tests. However, this has not resulted in the impoverishment of North Korea. In fact, since its first nuclear test in 2006, international trade has been growing and economic conditions appear to have improved steadily. North Korea's trade exceeded $7.3 billion in 2013, a 7.8 percent increase from the previous year and the highest since 1990 according to the Korea Trade-Investment Promotion Agency (KOTRA). Under the UN sanctions that allow most of the non-military economic transactions, China, in particular, has expanded economic exchanges with the North. In recent years, Russia has become more actively engaged with it. Seoul has not only maintained a certain level of economic interactions with it, but has also become more eager to expand them, while the United States and Japan have continued to impose strong unilateral sanctions against the North.

This chapter discusses the extent of economic engagement of the four major powers and South Korea with North Korea. More specifically, it examines the US reluctance to ease economic sanctions against North Korea, Japan's economic disengagement from North Korea after its first nuclear test, the reduction in South Korea's economic engagement during the Lee Myung Bak administration, the active economic engagement by China and Russia even after the third nuclear test, and the engagement policy of the Park Geun-hye administration. Finally, the author contemplates the future prospects of economic engagement.

THE US DISENGAGEMENT

Since the Korean War, the United States has imposed strong economic sanctions against the DPRK and has been reluctant to ease them and normalize relations. Economic engagement in terms of trade and investment has remained very low. The sanctions have hindered Pyongyang from obtaining investment and aid from other countries and international organizations, such as the World Bank and the Asian Development Bank (ADB). Not surprisingly, Pyongyang has urged Washington to end the sanctions and normalize relations with Pyongyang. Yet, Washington has been reluctant to do so. In the context of continuing hostile relations with Washington, Pyongyang has proceeded with nuclear and missile development.

Washington's unwillingness to normalize relations is understandable because diplomatic normalization with Pyongyang would likely reduce US influence in East Asia, particularly over Japan and South Korea. Normalization would lead to the DPRK's normalization with Japan and South Korea. That would reduce the importance of their military alliance with the United States. Normalization would also lead to a new phase of economic development in Northeast Asia and consequently decrease the economic importance of the United States to its two allies. For the United States, hostile relations with the DPRK remain useful in maintaining US influence over Japan and South Korea in dealing with the growing power of China. Therefore, Washington is likely to remain reluctant to ease economic sanctions against Pyongyang and to expand economic engagement.

JAPAN'S DISENGAGEMENT

Japan has shown more willingness than the United States to normalize relations with North Korea as can be seen from its initiation of normalization talks in 1991 and the Koizumi visits to Pyongyang in 2002 and 2004. However, deterioration of the nuclear and missile issues as well as the issue of the North's abduction of Japanese citizens have reduced domestic support for normalization in Japan.

There have not been many Japanese leaders who support improvement in Japan's relations with North Korea if doing so hurts its relations with the United States, which is widely seen in Japan as the most important country for Japan. This recognition has become even stronger in recent years as tension has risen between Japan and China over the Senkaku/Diaoyu Islands. Moreover, the politically dominant conservatives in Japan have been eager to ease the constitutional constraints on Japan's military activities to deal with North Korea and China. Finally, public support for diplomatic normalization with North Korea has been very limited because of strong anti–North Korea sentiment, resulting from North Korea's abduction of Japanese citizens and its problematic handling of the issue after admission of this during the first bilateral summit meeting in September 2002 as well as its nuclear and missile development.

After the first nuclear test in 2006, Tokyo unilaterally imposed economic sanctions against Pyongyang, including a trade embargo, which was significant because Japan had long been a major trade partner for North Korea. In May 2014, Tokyo agreed with Pyongyang to fully lift unilateral sanctions if Pyongyang conducts special investigations into the abduction and other issues involving Japanese citizens and fully resolves them. In July 2014, Tokyo eased its ban on travel and port calls and restriction on remittances in response to Pyongyang's establishment of a special investigation team.

However, it is highly unclear how much progress will be made from now on. In any case, given the continuing and even growing support for alliance with the US, Japan is unlikely to actively pursue diplomatic normalization with North Korea.

DECLINE IN SOUTH KOREA'S ENGAGEMENT

North Korea's renewed nuclear and missile development in response to the hardline policy of the Bush administration led to the end of the progressive administrations of Kim Dae Jung and Roh Moo Hyun, which had turned South Korea into the second biggest trade partner for the North and a leading provider of economic aid along with China, and resulted in the onset of the conservative administration of Lee Myung Bak, which made economic assistance to the North conditional upon denuclearization. Besides this, the killing of a South Korean woman during her participation in the Mount Kumgang tour in July 2008 led to suspension of the tour, which had been profitable for North Korea. Subsequently, the sinking of a South Korean corvette, *Cheonan*, during the ROK-US joint maritime exercise near the Northern Limit Line (NLL) in the Yellow Sea in March 2010 resulted in Seoul's imposition of economic sanctions against Pyongyang in May 2010 (5.24 sanctions), leaving the Kaesong Industrial Complex (KIC) as virtually the only major point of South Korea's economic engagement with the North.

Despite the scale-down in economic engagement since the onset of the Lee administration in 2008, South Korea has a greater potential to expand economic engagement than the United States and Japan. Compared to those two countries, there has been stronger support among the elite and the general public in South Korea for improving relations with the North. Just like the Japanese, many South Koreans look upon the United States as the most important country both militarily and economically. Yet, South Korea does not have territorial disputes with China as serious as Japan's. Nor does it face such constitutional constraints on military activities that Japan faces.

Furthermore, for South Korea, the importance of improving economic relations with North Korea is stronger than for Japan because of its greater economic dependence on international trade. South Korea can expect more economic benefit from expanding economic ties with the North and with China, Russia, and other Eurasian countries through the North. Thus, among the three countries that have confronted North Korea, South Korea has the greatest possibility to expand economic engagement. In fact, there have been changes in that direction under the current Park administration (which are analyzed later in the chapter), in the context of progress in the economic engagement of China and Russia, both of which seek economic benefit from expanding their economic relations with the North and from improvement in inter-Korea economic relations.

CHINA'S ENGAGEMENT

Since the end of the Cold War and the collapse of the Soviet Union, China has been economically supporting North Korea, preventing its collapse. China's aid to North Korea is believed to amount to $20 million per year, which includes 100,000 tons of food and 500,000 tons of oil.[1] China is not just an aid provider but is also the biggest trade partner for North Korea, accounting for as much as 89.1 percent of the North's trade when inter-Korea trade is excluded from the calculation, according to KOTRA. China's economic engagement goes beyond just preventing the North Korean regime from collapsing. China has also seen North Korea as an important source of natural resources, as a market, and as a logistics hub, particularly for its underdeveloped northeastern provinces.

For instance, in August 2009 its State Council officially approved the Changchun-Jilin-Tumen River Pilot Zone Development Project (2009–2020), which included a plan to strengthen the economic relations of China's northeastern provinces with North Korea's northern provinces. In May 2010 Kim Jong Il and President Hu Jintao met in Beijing and agreed to jointly build economic development zones in the border regions of the city of Rason and the Hwanggumphyong and Wihwa Islands in the city of Sinuiju.[2] Since then, China has upgraded transportation networks in the provinces and their access to the North Korean port of Rajin located in Rason.

For China, whose land territory is very close to the Sea of Japan but does not face it, Rajin can be a very important logistics hub for promoting economic development of the provinces, linking them not only to southern parts of China but also to South Korea, Japan, and other countries. The Chuangli Group of Dalian obtained the right to use No. 1 wharf of the Rajin port in 2008 and has already modernized it. In November 2011 the group started sending coal from the northeastern provinces of China into the Rajin port, shipping it out to Shanghai and other parts of the country, and has expanded the use of the port since.[3]

Furthermore, it is reported that China has already finished a preparatory survey for provision of electricity to Rason from China.[4] Improvement in the currently poor state of Rason's infrastructure would promote an inflow of Chinese companies into Rason, which has been limited to this date. Besides the port of Rajin, in September 2012 Yanbian Haihua Import-Export Trade Company signed a contract with the Chongjin Port Authority to upgrade the North Korean port of Chongjin. The company has renovated the port, and has started shipping goods out to China.[5]

North Korea's rocket launches in 2012 and the third nuclear test in 2013 soured its relations with China and apparently reduced Beijing's eagerness to assist North Korea's economic development, as can be seen from the suspension of oil exports to North Korea since January 2013 that was indicated in China's official trade statistics.[6] However, bilateral trade has continued to expand, with North Korea's export of natural resources and China's export of manufactured goods increasing, largely through the border cities of Sinuiju and Rason. Bilateral trade in 2013 reached $654.7 billion, 8.9 percent higher than in 2012.

Also, in March 2013 the Jilin provincial government announced plans to renovate the Tumen-Rajin railway and the Tumen-Chongjin railway.[7] Furthermore, it has been reported that on 24 February 2014 a Chinese consortium headed by the Shangdi Guanqun investment company and North Korea's State Economic Development Commission signed a contract for renovating the railway and constructing a highway linking Sinuiju with Chongju, Sukchon, Pyongyang, Haeju, and Kaesong, with the five-year construction beginning in 2018 and with a budget of $21 billion.[8] Besides this, on 9 December 2013, one day after the dismissal of Jang Song Taek, Kim Jong Un's uncle and the widely presumed No. 2 leader, the city of Tumen in Jilin Province reportedly signed the contract to develop the Onsong Economic Development Zone in North Hamkyung Province.[9] Furthermore, in May 2012, Beijing agreed with Seoul to assign preferential tariff status to those products made in the KIC by South Korean companies in their bilateral Free Trade Area (FTA) under negotiation, promoting further development of the KIC. Thus, China's economic engagement with North Korea is led not only by the central government but also by local governments and companies, particularly those in the northeastern provinces. Considering the continuing importance of the engagement, particularly for the provincial actors, further expansion seems highly likely.

RUSSIA'S ENGAGEMENT

Russia's economic engagement with the DPRK has been much smaller than China's. As of 2013, Russia was North Korea's third biggest trade partner, with the bilateral trade standing at approximately $104.2 million according to KOTRA. However, economic engagement has become more active in recent years, even after the third nuclear test. Russia's exports to North Korea increased by 48.6 percent in 2013 from the previous year according to KOTRA, and further expansion seems likely. The Russian government has been pushing for strengthening its economic ties with Northeast Asian countries to stimulate the economy of its underdeveloped Far Eastern region and thereby revitalize the national economy.[10] Moscow has been eager to expand trade with countries in the region and turn Russia into a major trade route between Northeast Asia and Europe.[11] As can be seen from the establishment of the Ministry for Development of the Russian Far East in May 2012, this has been more conspicuous particularly after the onset of the global financial crisis in 2007 that resulted in a decline in Russian exports of natural resources to Europe, and after the start of large-scale production of shale gas particularly by the United States, which has weakened Russia's price-setting power vis-à-vis the present and prospective importers of its gas.

Russia has already discussed various projects with the two Koreas and has gained their support, including the connection of Russian railways, gas pipelines, and power grids to South Korea's through North Korea. All three parties can benefit from these projects. President Medvedev agreed to promote the gas pipelines project with President Lee in September 2008. He made a similar agreement with General Secretary Kim Jong Il in August 2011 during Kim's first visit to Russia since 2002, while also agreeing to resolve the issue of North Korea's outstanding debt to Russia. Although these trilateral projects have not made much progress due to the volatile relations between the two Koreas, Russia has not lost its willingness to push them forward even after North Korea's third nuclear test. Also, it has explored other ways to profit from its economic engagement with North Korea.

Russia's determination to pursue its economic interests by strengthening economic ties with North Korea can be seen from its decision in September 2012 to write off 90 percent of Pyongyang's Soviet-era $11 billion debt to Moscow, which was ratified by the State Duma lower house in April 2014. The remaining $1.09 billion is to be paid back in equal installments every six months over the next twenty years.[12] Apparently, the debt deal was Russia's strategic move to advance its economic interests vis-à-vis North Korea, in particular to make Pyongyang more committed to the trilateral projects that Russia has pursued and to help its mining industry operate in North Korea. This is evident in remarks in April 2014 by Russia's Deputy Finance Minister Sergei Storchak to the effect that the money could be used to fund mutual projects in North Korea, including a proposed gas pipeline and a railway to South Korea.[13]

Also in April 2014, Russia and the DPRK signed an economic development protocol pertaining to cooperation in trade, investment, transport, energy and natural resources, employment, and interregional cooperation at their meeting in Rason. At the meeting, they agreed to aim at expanding their annual bilateral trade to $1 billion by the year 2020.[14] The Russian Ministry of Far East Development expressed its eagerness to complete a trans-Siberian railway connection to South Korea that could facilitate its supply of gas and electricity to the South through the North.[15] Also, the Russian delegation to the meeting expressed Russia's interest in establishing trilateral economic ties and its intentions to invest in the KIC,[16] which would reduce the perceived risks of investing in North Korea and promote further investment by South Korean companies.

In June 2014 Russia and North Korea held another meeting in Vladivostok and reached an agreement on over a dozen trade and economic development projects, including Russia's participation in gold mine development in North Korea in exchange for its provision of secondhand Tu-204 aircrafts, and conclusion of conventions pertaining to their joint project of building a gas station network in North Korea led by Russia's TAIF petrochemical company.[17] At the meeting, North Korea expressed its expectation of the participation of Russian firms in exploration of minerals, including copper, quartzite, vanadium anhydride, and ultra-anthracite deposits,[18] indicating its desire to reduce North Korea's excessive dependence on Chinese companies. Aside from this agreement, in March 2014 the President of the Russian Republic of Tatarstan, Rustam Minnikhanov, visited Pyongyang to discuss joint exploration and development of petroleum gas fields in North Korea.[19]

To facilitate Russian investment, North Korea agreed to simplify procedures for Russians to obtain and use multiple-entry visas for business purposes and to allow them to use the Internet and mobile phones in North Korea.[20] On the series of agreements reached at the June meeting, Alexander Galushka, the Russian Far East Development Minister, told the media that "the North Korean Government has allowed this agreement exclusively for Russian entrepreneurs and that overseas investors, including those from China, have not enjoyed such benefits to date."[21]

Besides these agreements, in a manner similar to China, Russia has attempted to use Rajin as its logistics hub. In fact, in 2008 Russia and North Korea started renovating No. 3 wharf of the Rajin port and upgrading the fifty-four-kilometer railway between Rajin and Khasan (in Russia), which was originally agreed in 2001. For the joint project, in 2008 a joint venture, RasonKonTrans, was established with Russian Railways contributing 70 percent of its capital and the Rason Port Authority, 30 percent. Russian Railways invested 9 billion rubles ($250 million) to upgrade the wharf and the railways.[22] In December 2011 Pyongyang enacted an international railroad cargo law, the first of its kind, apparently in preparation for its transactions with Russia and China.[23]

Russia and North Korea held an official opening ceremony in September 2013 upon completion of renovation of the wharf and the railway. The new multipurpose facility at the terminal in the Rajin port has a cargo traffic capacity of about five million tons a year and the capacity for coal magnetic cleaning and coal separating.[24] For political and economic reasons, completion of trilateral train connections between Russia and South Korea via North Korea would take many years. For the time being, Russia can use the Rajin port as a gateway to other counties, particularly China, and possibly South Korea and Japan, supplementary to the existing ports in the Russian Far East such as Vladivostok, which face congestion.[25] In fact, Russia has already begun its use of the Rajin port, sending out its first shipment of a total of 9,000 metric tons of coal at the end of March 2014 to the final destinations of Shanghai, Lianyungang, and Guangzhou in China via the port.[26]

Considering possible further decline in Russia's gas and other exports to Europe due to its confrontation with the European Union and the United States over its annexation of Crimea and its involvement in the conflict in Ukraine, Russia may well make greater efforts to expand its economic engagement with North Korea in order to expand its exports, to profit from its investment in North Korea, and to use North Korea as a logistics hub.

THE PARK ADMINISTRATION'S ENGAGEMENT

Park Geun-hye, who comes from the same party to which Lee Myung Bak belonged, took office on 25 February 2013 and adopted a North Korea policy that is similar to that of Lee, maintaining the 5.24 sanctions against North Korea that Lee instituted in May 2010 and making South Korea's provision of large-scale economic assistance to the North conditional upon its denuclearization. Just before and after the onset of the Park administration, Pyongyang conducted its third nuclear test on 12 February and withdrew all North Korean workers from the KIC in April 2013, using a joint ROK-US military drill as a pretext.

However, compared to Lee, Park has been more eager to improve inter-Korea relations and expand economic engagement for that purpose. Her eagerness can be attributed to: (1) South Korea's structural need to enhance its economic competitiveness as discussed above, (2) the failure of Lee's hardline policy toward North Korea to improve inter-Korea relations and to promote the North's denuclearization, (3) the economic success of the KIC, (4) the progress of China and Russia's economic engagement with the North, and (5) Kim Jong Un's eagerness to expand North Korea's international economic relations.

With regard to the KIC, President Park decided not to permanently shut it down despite Pyongyang's outrageous unilateral withdrawal of the workers. This is partly because the South Korean companies at the KIC were doing well, taking advantage of the cheap, diligent North Korean workers. Production expanded even after the 5.24 sanctions that froze the establishment of businesses by new companies at the KIC. There have been significant calls from business circles, particularly small and medium-sized businesses, for the establishment of additional industrial complexes in North Korea, even after the shocking withdrawal.[27] The operations of the KIC resumed in September 2014. Consequently, South Korea remains the North's second biggest trade partner, with their bilateral trade standing at $1.1 billion in 2013 according to the ROK Unification Ministry.

In October 2013 Park proposed the "Eurasia Initiative." In the initiative, she advocated connecting logistics networks, linking energy infrastructure including electricity grids, gas and oil pipelines, and co-developing China's shale gas and eastern Siberia's petroleum and gas.[28] As a part of the connection of logistics networks, she proposed establishment of a "Silk Road Express" that would connect rail and road networks from South Korea's Busan to Europe via North Korea.

Park intends to utilize the Eurasia Initiative to build trust between the two Koreas, as can be seen from her North Korea policy which is called the "Korean Peninsula Trust-Building Process." The process entails economic engagement with North Korea in three stages: (1) humanitarian assistance such as food aid, (2) low-level economic cooperation in such fields as agriculture and forestry, and (3) large-scale investment in projects to develop infrastructure such as transportation and communication. It is notable that the Park administration has shown willingness to implement the first two stages without making North Korea's denuclearization a precondition.[29]

As a concrete step in accordance with the Eurasia Initiative and the Korean Peninsula Trust-Building Process, in November 2013 President Park and President Putin agreed to strengthen their efforts to implement a trans-Korean/trans-Siberian railroad, which could significantly reduce freight times between the Far East and Europe.[30] As a first step, they agreed that three major South Korean firms (Korea Railroad Corporation, Hyundai Merchant Marine, and POSCO, one of the biggest steel companies in the world) would take part in Russia's project with North Korea to improve Russia's railway access from Hassan to Rajin and modernize the port of Rajin, in the form of the three firms' contribution to Russia's capital share of RasonKonTrans. As a starter, the companies intended to ship Russian coal to the port of Pohang by the end of 2014, where POSCO has a major steel factory.[31] This development is particularly noteworthy because it amounts to virtual easing of the 5.24 sanctions. Seoul allowed an eighteen-member delegation of the three companies to visit Rason in February 2014, which was followed by another thirty-eight-member delegation including government officials in July 2014. Pyongyang unofficially welcomed Seoul's involvement in its joint project with Moscow.[32] It should be noted that POSCO and Hyundai have been constructing a 150-square-meter international logistics complex in Hunchun, China, 53 kilometers away from Rajin since September 2012. Their involvement in the two projects indicates their strong intention to build a logistics network in the three-nation border region.

In March 2014, in her speech at the Dresden University of Technology, Park again expressed her eagerness to conduct active economic engagement with the North, not only to improve the humanitarian situation there but also to promote South Korea's economic interests, in addition to making an effort to restore a sense of common nationhood as a basis for Korean unification. She stressed the mutual benefits that both parties can expect from South Korea's development of North Korea's natural resources, arguing that "[t]his would organically combine South Korean capital and technology with North Korean resources and labor and redound to the eventual formation of an economic community on the Korean Peninsula."[33] She went on, expressing her intention to "push forward collaborative projects involving both Koreas and China centered on the North Korean city of Shinuiju, among others… [I]n tandem with trilateral projects among the two Koreas and Russia, including the Rajin-Khasan joint project currently in the works."[34]

Following the Dresden Speech, in August 2014 the ROK Ministry of Unification announced a comprehensive inter-Korea development program for Seoul to pursue, which was the first detailed plan for large-scale infrastructure investments.[35] The program included: Kaesong-Sinuiju railway and Kaesong-Pyongyang expressway repairs, Imjin River flood prevention, support for North Korea's fishing industry, vitalization of inter-Korea shipping, and gradual resumption of trade and commerce depending on the progress in improvement in inter-Korea relations. Furthermore, on 18 September 2014, the Export-Import Bank of Korea signed an agreement with its Chinese, Russian, and Mongolian counterparts to launch the Northeast Asia EXIM Banks Association to cooperate in financing joint development projects in Northeast Asia, and expressed its resolve to take the lead in promoting such projects in the region.[36]

Although Pyongyang denounced the Dresden Speech,[37] it is quite possible that it would allow South Korea to take part in the China-DPRK joint projects of Kaesong-Sinuiju railway and Kaesong-Pyongyang expressway repairs, considering its support for South Korea's participation of the Rajin-Khasan project, its participation in the 2014 Asian Games held in Incheon, and its dispatch of three of its highest-ranking officials to Incheon on 4 October 2014—the vice chairman of the National Defense Commission and Director of the General Political Bureau Hwang Pyong So, believed to be the No. 2 after Kim Jong Un; Secretary of the Central Committee of the Workers' Party Choe Ryong Hae, believed to the former No. 2; and Director of the United Front Department Kim Yang Gon—who were greeted by the ROK Unification Minister Ryoo Kihl Jae and National Security Director Kim Kwan Jin.

CONCLUSION

Compared to the United States and Japan, China, Russia, and South Korea have considered North Korea as more important to their economic development. Hence, this explains their more active economic engagement with North Korea. As discussed above, North Korea's structural attributes, particularly its geographic location, natural resource endowment, and its cheap, diligent, and sizable working population make it attractive to these three countries. For North Korea, it remains important to improve its poor economic conditions and thereby enhance its regime stability through international economic exchanges. In fact, Pyongyang under the leadership of Kim Jong Un has been very active in promoting economic development and improving economic conditions of the North Korean people. This can be seen from Kim Jong Un's New Year addresses in 2013 and 2014 in which he gave precedence to economic development and from the actual policy measures he has taken.

For instance, in October 2013 Pyongyang decided to establish thirteen more special economic zones (SEZs) and has made administrative changes in order to attract foreign investment in North Korea.[38] It also decided to create a high-tech industrial park in Kaesong, near the KIC. In November 2013 construction of the park was started by the Peace Economic Development Group, a consortium of foreign investors from Hong Kong, Singapore, Australia, the Middle East, and Africa.[39]

In June 2014 North Korea merged the Joint Venture and Investment Commission and the State Economic Development Commission into a new Ministry of External Economic Affairs, thereby unifying the divided authorities to manage SEZs. In July 2014 it announced six new SEZs, including the Unjong technology development zone in Pyongyang and the Kangryong international green model zone in a military foothold near the Northern Limit Line (NLL). Opening up these militarily important areas to foreign investment indicates Pyongyang's seriousness in promoting economic development. It has also eased the government control of the economy, giving farmers and managers greater autonomy. There have been reports of increase in production in the agricultural and manufacturing sectors.

Paradoxically, Pyongyang's greater focus on economic development resulted from its success in the satellite launch in December 2012 and the third nuclear test in February 2013. Its nuclear and missile development has reached the stage where Kim Jong Un can say to the North Korean people and the military that his country has achieved the goal of becoming a militarily strong state and that its next goal is to become an economically strong state. Thus, the military development has given North Korea's leadership an opportunity to shift its priority from military to economic development.

Success of the ongoing economic reforms would enhance the relative power of the reformists vis-à-vis the conservatives within the Kim Jong Un regime, and would thereby increase the chance of continuation and expansion of economic reforms. Considering the convergence of economic interests among North Korea, China, Russia, and South Korea, North Korea's economic interactions with these countries are likely to continue and may well expand not only bilaterally but also multilaterally, as can be seen from South Korea's participation in the Rajin-Khasan joint project.

If further expansion of the economic engagement by China, Russia, and South Korea improves North Korea's economic conditions and increases North Korea's eagerness to maintain and expand its profitable economic relations with them, this might reduce the risk of Pyongyang selling its nuclear technologies and materials to other countries or terrorists. Also, engagement expansion might make North Korea more willing to refrain from making provocations such as conducting another nuclear test—although this would not necessarily stop North Korea's weapons development, which is aimed at countering the continuing economic and military pressures from the United States, as can be seen from its nuclear and missile development in the context of expanding economic interactions with China and South Korea. Furthermore, if the third nuclear test was as successful as Pyongyang claims, then the military need for a fourth test is not very strong. Considering these factors, there is a good chance for further expansion of North Korea's economic interactions with China, Russia, and South Korea.

If South Korea, prompted by the economic engagement of China and Russia, fully lifts its 5.24 sanctions and reaps more profits from greater economic engagement with the North, then Japan may well find it increasingly disadvantageous to maintain its trade embargo on the North. In fact, the Japan-DPRK agreement in May 2014 can be seen in this light—that is, as Tokyo's attempt to restart its economic engagement. Although the North Korea nuclear issue and the US economic sanctions against the North likely continue to limit the economic engagement of South Korea and Japan, the two countries may seek to expand the engagement within the limitations.

NOTES

1. Nagoshi Kenrō, "Kitachousen to Roshia 'kyūsekkin' no fukai wake [The underlying reason behind the rapid improvement in North Korea-Russia relations]," *Foresight*, 23 June 2014, accessed 15 September 2014, http://www .fsight.jp/27498.

2. For details on the projects, see Choi Myeong-Hae, "The DPRK-PRC Joint Projects in Rason and Hwanggumpyong," *SERI Quarterly*, 1 October 2011, 130–36.

3. "Konshun ga kokusai butsuryu daitsūro o kouchiku e [Hunchun, building major international logistics routes]," Official Government Website of Jilin Province, 12 August 2014, accessed 15 September 2014, http://japanese .jl.gov.cn/xw/201408/t20140812_1714674.html.

4. Charlie Zhu, "China moves ahead with North Korea trade zone despite nuclear test," Reuters, 28 February 2013, accessed 20 October 2014, http:// www.reuters.com/article/2013/03/01/us-china-northkorea-trade -idUSBRE92005I20130301.

5. Kim Young-jin, "China Extends Influence to N. Korea's Chongjin Port," *Korea Times*, 11 September 2012, accessed 15 September 2014, http://www .koreatimes.co.kr/www/news/nation/2012/09/113_119673.html.

6. There have been views that question the actual suspension, though. "DPRK Oil Imports from China in 2014 (UPDATED)," *North Korean Economy Watch*, 23 August 2014, accessed 15 September 2014, http://www .nkeconwatch.com/category/international-trade/.

7. Wang Zhaokun, "China-North Korea Railway Links to Undergo Upgrade," *Global Times*, 27 March 2013, http://www.globaltimes.cn/content/770938 .shtml#.UVIEGpNwqSo.

8. "Sinuiju-Kaesong High-Speed Rail Project (UPDATED)," *North Korean Economy Watch*, 29 April 2014, accessed 15 September 2014, http://www .nkeconwatch.com/2014/04/07/high-speed-rail-and-road-connecting -kaesong-pyongyang-sinuiju-to-be-built/.

9. Sun Xiaobo and Park Gayoung, "N. Korea Inks Border Town Economic Deal," *Global Times*, 13 December 2013, accessed 15 September 2014, http:// www.globaltimes.cn/content/831869.shtml#.UsWXH9JDtHU.

10. Alexander Fedorovskiy, "Russia's Policy Toward North Korea," *Russian Analytical Digest*, no. 132 (11 July 2013): 5–6.

11. Ole Jakob Skåtun, "Russian Vice-Premier Visits Pyongyang to Discuss Economic Ties," *NK News*, 28 April 2014, accessed 17 September 2014, http://www.nknews.org/2014/04/russian-vice-premier-heads-to-pyongyang-to-discuss-economic-ties/.

12. "Russia Writes Off 90 Percent of North Korea Debt, Eyes Gas Pipeline," Reuters, 19 April 2014, accessed 17 September 2014, http://www.reuters.com/article/2014/04/19/uk-russia-northkorea-debt-idINKBN0D502V20140419.

13. Ibid.

14. Kang Tae-jun, "Russia Signs Economic Development Protocol with North Korea," *NK News*, 3 April 2014, accessed 17 September 2014, http://www.nknews.org/2014/04russia-signs-economic-development-protocol-with-north-korea/.

15. Ibid.

16. Ibid.

17. "North Korea-Russia: Expanding Economic Ties," *KGS NightWatch*, 11 June 2014, accessed 17 September 2014, http://www.kforcegov.com/NightWatch/NightWatch_14000124.aspx.

18. Ibid.

19. Skåtun, "Russian Vice-Premier Visits Pyongyang."

20. "North Korea-Russia."

21. Ibid.

22. Anatoly Medetsky, "First Russian Coal Heads to North Korean Port," *Moscow Times*, 8 April 2014, accessed 17 September 2014, http://www.themoscowtimes.com/business/article/first-russian-coal-heads-to-north-korean-port/497748.html.

23. "International Railroad Cargo Law Passed," *IFES*, November 8, 2013, accessed 17 September 2014, http://ifes.kyungnam.ac.kr/eng/FRM/FRM_0101V.aspx?code=FRM131108_0001.

24. "North Korea Launches Russian-Korean Terminal in Rason Economic Zone," ITAR-TASS, 18 July 2013, accessed 17 September 2014, http://en.itar-tass.com/economy/741383.

25. Medetsky, "First Russian Coal."

26. Ibid.

27. "SME Federation Chief Mentions 2nd Inter-Korean Industrial Complex," *Dong-A Ilbo*, 25 July 2014, accessed 21 September 2014, http://english.donga.com/srv/service.php3?biid=2014072598778.

28. "Park Seeks 'Eurasia Initiative' to Build Energy, Logistics Links," *Korea Herald*, 18 October 2013, accessed 21 September 2014, http://www.koreaherald.com /view.php?ud=20131018000620.

29. The Ministry of Unification, *Trust-Building Process on the Korean Peninsula* (Seoul: Ministry of Unification, September 2013), 16–17; "S. Korea to Delink Humanitarian Aid from N. Korea's Denuclearization Actions," Yonhap News Agency, 27 March 2013, accessed 20 October 2014, http://english.yonhapnews .co.kr/national/2013/03/27/34/0301000000AEN20130327001800315F .HTML.

30. Skåtun, "Russian Vice-Premier Visits Pyongyang."

31. "N. Korea Willing to Host S. Korean Investment in Rajin-Khasan Project: Official," Yonhap News Agency, 24 July2014, accessed 21 September 2014, http://english.yonhapnews.co.kr/national/2014/07/24/88/0301000000AEN2 0140724007600315F.html.

32. Ibid.

33. Ibid.

34. Park Geun-hye, "An Initiative for Peaceful Unification on the Korean Peninsula - Dresden Speech," *National Unification Advisory Council*, April 2014, accessed 21 September 2014, http://www.nuac.go.kr/japanese/sub04 /view01.jsp?numm=279.

35. Koo Jun Hoe, "Report: 2014 Inter-Korean Development Plans," *Daily NK*, 19 August 2014, accessed 21 September 2014, http://www.dailynk.com /english/read.php?num=12223&cataId=nk00100.

36. Choi Kyong-ae, "Korea Eximbank Seeks Lead in Northeast Asia's Development," *Korea Times*, 29 September 2014, accessed 30 September 2014, http://koreatimes.co.kr/www/news/biz/2014/09/488_165441.html.

37. "NDC Spokesman Blasts Park Geun Hye's 'Dresden Declaration,' KCNA, 12 April 2014, accessed 21 September 2014, http://www.kcna.co.jp/item /2014/201404/news12/20140412-01ee.html.

38. "Kitachousen, Keizai Tokku 14kasho shinsetsu [North Korea Establishing 14 New Special Economic Zones]," *Asahi Shimbun*, 28 October 2013: 7; "Gunji kyoukai sen chikakuni tokku" [A Special Economic Zone Near the DMZ], *Asahi Shimbun*, 6 November 2013: 11.

39. "High-Tech Industrial Park to Be Built in Kaesong," KCNA, 13 November 2013, accessed 25 September 2014, http://www.kcna.co.jp/item/2013/201311 /news13/20131113-17ee.html.

CHAPTER 6

The North Korea Problem from South Korea's Perspective

Jihwan HWANG

What national interests of South Korea are involved in the North Korea problem? What recently embarrasses South Korea most in this regard is that as North Korea's dependence on China gets bigger, its dependence on South Korea gets smaller. North Korea's increasing dependence on China is in part a natural result of China's rise in East Asia,[1] but it is also because North Korea is deliberately relying less on South Korea. This situation must mean that while China's influence on North Korea is growing, South Korea's influence is getting weaker. As Robert O. Keohane and Joseph S. Nye Jr. explain,[2] asymmetric interdependence can be the origin of power. It implies that as North Korea's sensitivity and vulnerability to China are getting larger, so is China's influence on North Korea.

Table 1 and Table 2 indicate that North Korea's economic dependence on South Korea has been decreasing or static since 2008, when President Lee Myung Bak took office.[3] While North Korea's trade with South Korea has been increasing overall (though somewhat fluctuating), the rate of the rise has stagnated since 2008. The Lee Myung Bak government (2008–2013) dramatically reduced South Korea's economic aid to North Korea.[4] These data clearly mean that North Korea has become economically less dependent on South Korea than before, which implies that South Korea's economic influence on North Korea is weakening.

Table 1. North Korea's Trade with South Korea (million US dollars)

Year	2005	2006	2007	2008	2009	2010	2011	2012	2013
Exports	340	520	765	932	934	1,044	914	1,074	615
Imports	715	830	1,032	888	745	868	800	897	521
Total	1,055	1,350	1,798	1,820	1,679	1,912	1,714	1,971	1,136

Source: Ministry of Unification, Republic of Korea

Table 2. South Korea's Economic Aid to North Korea (billion Korean won)

Year	2005	2006	2007	2008	2009	2010	2011	2012	2013
Governmental	314.7	227.3	348.8	43.8	29.4	20.4	6.5	2.3	13.5
Nongovernmental	77.9	70.9	90.9	72.5	37.7	20.0	13.1	11.8	5.1
Total	392.6	298.2	439.7	116.3	67.1	40.4	19.6	14.1	18.6

Source: Ministry of Unification, Republic of Korea

Conversely, Table 3 shows that North Korea's economic dependence on China is growing quickly. North Korea's trade with China more than doubled during the Lee Myung Bak government, and is likely to be increasing continuously. In reality, North Korea has recently made up for the decrement from South Korea with an increment from China. North Korea is thus now economically much more dependent on China than on South Korea, which will lead to a difference in economic influence on North Korea.

Table 3. North Korea's Trade with China (million US dollars)

Year	2005	2006	2007	2008	2009	2010	2011	2012
Exports	496	467	581	754	1,887	1,187	2,464	2,480
Imports	1,084	1,231	1,392	2,033	793	2,277	3,165	3,530
Total	1,580	1,698	1,973	2,787	2,680	3,464	5,629	6,010

Source: Korea Trade-Investment Promotion Agency (KOTRA), Republic of Korea

Of course, the growing Chinese influence but weakening South Korean influence on North Korea has not just occurred in the economic area. Chinese influence is also much stronger in diplomatic and military areas.[5]

If South Korea wants to have as much control over affairs on the Korean Peninsula in an era of a changing balance of power as it had for the last two decades since the early 1990s, South Korea itself should make every effort to enlarge its influence over North Korea. The security environment favorable to South Korea around the Korean Peninsula mainly resulted from the US preponderance of power in East Asia after the end of the Cold War, but the balance of power in the region appears to be changing again and has become less advantageous for South Korea.[6] South Korea cannot safeguard its own national interests without increasing its influence on North Korea.

THE SOUTH KOREA DEBATE: CONSERVATIVES VS. LIBERALS

There is a serious debate between conservatives and liberals in South Korea about how to deal with North Korea. Liberals expect that Pyongyang may be willing to give up the nuclear option or that it has been simply using the nuclear issue to gain concessions from the United States and South Korea. Conservatives do not believe that North Korea will voluntarily sacrifice its nuclear weapons program for any reason. In their view, Pyongyang perceives keeping nuclear weapons as a vital interest and therefore the apparent willingness of the DPRK to offer concessions was merely a stalling tactic. Conservatives say North Korea is determined to possess its nuclear weapons regardless of any security assurances. Given the seriousness of the North Korea nuclear crisis, Pyongyang may well feel that possession of nuclear weapons is a better guarantee against US nuclear strikes than any other verbal security guarantees that the United States and South Korea may offer. In this perspective, North Korea is not likely to voluntarily give up its nuclear weapons.

Some conservatives argue that North Korea has sought to reunify the Korean Peninsula with its nuclear weapons program. They say that given the North's record of aggressive behavior, acquiring nuclear weapons will reinforce Pyongyang's inclination to invade the South. Even if Pyongyang's nuclear capability were used only as a deterrent against the US nuclear threat, the dangerousness of North Korea as a rogue state would inevitably increase. Thus, these conservatives are skeptical of the notion that Pyongyang's intentions have changed from offensive to defensive.

Liberals, however, argue that North Korea can be persuaded or bought off to suspend its nuclear weapons program if the United States and South Korea guarantee its security and offer appropriate economic rewards.[7] Because North Korea may give up its nuclear weapons under certain circumstances, they believe that the North Korea nuclear issue is an "avoidable crisis." Thus, they argue that negotiations should be done on the assumption that Pyongyang might be "talked down" from its defiant nuclear posture. They do not deny that North Korea wishes to develop nuclear weapons for its security. It is not unreasonable to them that any nation with intense security concerns such as those of North Korea should wish to possess nuclear weapons. Furthermore, they recognize that the nuclear program became a useful tool of diplomacy and a flexible support system by drawing world attention to Pyongyang and establishing a firmer power basis for the regime. North Korea's significance to the world with the bomb is much greater than it is without the bomb. Thus, liberals believe that the North Korea nuclear program can be shut down if Pyongyang's security concerns and economic difficulties are addressed. Because North Korea's goal is regime survival, not a military confrontation with the United States and South Korea, liberals argue, the nuclear weapons program is intended as a deterrent and a bargaining chip to ensure the survival of the regime. To them, although North Korea is not the most reliable negotiating partner and may even cheat if it is allowed to, it is likely to give up most, if not all, of its nuclear capabilities and engage the international community peacefully, as long as its security concerns are addressed and it feels that the long-term military and economic benefit outweighs the short-term benefit of developing nuclear weapons.

The Kim Dae Jung and Roh Moo Hyun governments supported the liberal view and energetically pursued negotiation with the North. Conversely, the Lee Myung Bak and Park Geun-hye governments acted according to the conservative perspective.

HOW DO WE RESOLVE THE NORTH KOREA PROBLEM?

What kind of solution would best suit South Korea's national interests? The North Korea issue may not be one that can be solved simply by changing the policy of the international community or of the South Korea government. Previous South Korea governments lacked programs that, even if successful, had the ability to transform the nature of the North Korean regime. The possibility of the North's leadership promoting a reform program along the lines of the Chinese or Vietnamese model is low due to North Korea's domestic situation and the security environment on the Korean Peninsula. South Korea's policymaking should focus on how to lead North Korea's leadership to pursue its own interests through means that are compatible with a peaceful relationship with Seoul.[8]

If North Korea's leaders began trying to reform their system, the immediate result would be heightened socioeconomic instability due to the loosened grip on internal politics, so the DPRK leaders would feel increasingly threatened by their relative weakness compared to South Korea.[9] Therefore for the successful resolution of the North Korea issue, there must be a linked internal-external strategy that consists of North Korea both giving up its nuclear weapons and promoting an economic reform program, while South Korea and the international society simultaneously ensure and support the safety of this policy.[10] This is why South Korea's government should create a new North Korea policy that increases the South's leverage on the North's perception and decision-making procedure. A new policy should also seek to engage both the United States and China.

The discussions of a peace regime on the Korean Peninsula will be limited and ineffective unless recent changes in international relations are considered. A broad format such as the previous Six-Party Talks is necessary and should account for the changing balance of power between the United States and China. The difficulty here, however, is crafting a strategy that can succeed in the absence of trust between the two great powers around the Korean Peninsula.

Advocating a new policy of engaging both the United States and China in a solution to the North Korea crisis may seem reckless and unrealistic, but the current environment surrounding the Korean Peninsula is actually quite favorable for implementing such a new policy despite the apparent difficulties. It becomes clearer if we understand that North Korea is facing a three-fold crisis of nuclear, economic, and leadership problems, while its external behavior burdens China. Thus, resolving the North Korea problem requires fundamental reform in all sectors including politics, international relations, the economy, and the socio-cultural realm as well as the nuclear issue.[11] In order to produce a new North Korea policy, South Korea's government should find out how to lead North Korea to achieve fundamental reform and abandon its Songun (military-first) policy, which puts first priority on the military sector, as well as the Byungjin (in tandem) policy that seeks to develop nuclear weapons capability and the economy simultaneously. South Korea cannot depend on China's influence on North Korea to achieve this task. Given North Korea's political situation, unless change in the political structure comes first, there is a very low chance that nuclear weapons will be given up and economic reforms will be carried out. China, however, is unlikely to seek to change North Korea's political structure because this is a sovereignty issue.

In this context, it is necessary that South Korea's government aim to make North Korea decide its strategy regarding nuclear weapons and economic reforms during its process of achieving the regime stability.

Turning Pyongyang from a "military-first policy" to an "economy-first policy" cannot be done by Chinese influence, but can be done through South Korea's influence on North Korea. This is why South Korea's government should pursue a North Korea policy that strengthens ROK's leverage over North Korea.

Given the changing balance of power on the Korean Peninsula, it is also necessary to resolve the problem of "excess security" caused by the military tension between the two Koreas. In order to achieve this difficult task, South Korea should come up with a new North Korea policy that would increase the North's dependence on the South. The first step for this is to rethink the changes in the balance of power after the end of US unipolarity in world politics and to take advantage of the changing relationship between the United States and China.[12]

THE UNITED STATES, CHINA, AND
SOUTH KOREA'S FOREIGN POLICY

In bargaining or negotiating with other countries regarding the North Korea problem, what would be the minimum that South Korea demands? After Kim Jong Il's sudden death in December 2011, North Korea has been more dependent on China as the new leadership cannot help but seek China's support in order to stabilize North Korean society. However, it is not in South Korea's interest to let North Korea keep increasing its dependence on China and let China keep increasing its influence over North Korea. China's growing influence over North Korea will inevitably lead to its leverage on the whole Korean Peninsula and also affect South Korea–China relations, not only with regard to the North Korea issue but also with regard to South Korea's strategic choice between the United States and China. Some may argue that even the changing balance of power between the United States and China does not challenge South Korea's strategic choice in the post–Cold War security environment in East Asia because the Obama administration's declaration that the United States is an Asia-Pacific country and pursuit of a "pivot to Asia" or "rebalancing" toward East Asia compensate for the rise of relative Chinese power.[13] The changes in the balance of power in East Asia result not only from the relative decline of the United States, but also from China's rapid increase in military and economic power. Thus, if South Korea wants to keep its initiative on the Korean Peninsula in spite of the changing balance of power in East Asia, it needs to balance against China's influence over North Korea. In order to balance against China's influence, South Korea should seek to enlarge its influence over North Korea by encouraging the North to depend more and more on the South Korean side.

However, North Korea will be very reluctant to increase its dependence on South Korea under such a changing balance of power because the rise of China and the decline of the United States in East Asia create a less favorable security environment for North Korea compared with the post–Cold War framework, it is more likely to avoid the further increase of South Korean and US influence. North Korea, of course, would not want to be under excessive Chinese influence either, but it will seek to make use of China to confront South Korea and the United States. In short, North Korea will build up its negotiating capability by taking advantage of the new balance of power in East Asia. For example, as shown in the cases of the sinking of the South Korean corvette *Cheonan* and the shelling of Yeonpyeong Island in 2010, North Korea will try to escalate the tension between the United States and China regarding the issues of the Korean Peninsula. If the Six-Party Talks resume in the future after their long period of suspension since December 2008, North Korea is more likely to insist on its demands and to stand firm by highlighting the conflict between the positions of the United States and China.

In order to cope with the changing balance of power in East Asia and North Korea's new balancing behavior, South Korea must make every effort to enlarge its common perspective with China. South Korea should demand that the United States and China meet together to talk about the future of North Korea and the Korean Peninsula. A significant challenge will be persuading the United States and China to share their perceptions and policy preferences with South Korea. If China perceives South Korea to be a more important player than North Korea in East Asia, it will be easier to persuade China to rethink the denuclearization and reunification of the Korean Peninsula, which will serve not only Korean but also China's interests in the long run. Given the importance of asymmetric interdependence as a source of power, South Korea should seek to upgrade Korea-China relations and cause China to depend more on South Korea not only economically but also strategically, because China's influence on the South as well as on the North will grow if North Korea's dependence on China increases asymmetrically.

On the other hand, it is necessary for South Korea to lead North Korea to depend more on South Korea than on China. If North Korea is getting more dependent on South Korea, South Korea will have more leverage on the issues of the Korean Peninsula and it will be easier to persuade China to agree to South Korean initiatives. Increasing South Korea's influence on North Korea while decreasing China's influence is how South Korea should respond to the rise of China in East Asia.

It is important to know what areas of South Korea's position regarding North Korea are negotiable, and could possibly be compromised in order to reach agreements with other countries in the region on a common approach to dealing with North Korea. In this regard, South Korea may guarantee the security of North Korea in the early phase of North Korea's transformation from military-first politics into economy-first politics in order to build mutual trust. This guarantee would involve not only protecting against external threats to North Korea but also maintaining domestic security under the Kim Jong Un leadership. Signing the North Korea–US peace treaty that North Korea is demanding in return for the abandonment of its nuclear weapons and the nonaggression pact by the United States and South Korea can be considered as a possible way to guarantee the security of North Korea. In addition, the establishment of liaison offices could lay the groundwork for the normalization of North Korea–US and North Korea–Japan relations. Most importantly, establishing US liaison offices in North Korea has been discussed several times, the 1994 Geneva Agreed Framework being the most representative case. Improvements in North Korea–US and North Korea–Japan relations may be necessary to resolve problems related to excessive security and excessive military concerns, and also be acceptable to South Korea.

China's active guarantee of the security of North Korea would be a daring way to increase North Korea's perception of safety from external threats. After the early 1990s, North Korea's fear of external threats has rapidly increased since the former Soviet Union collapsed and China lost its status as a security patron of North Korea in the process of systemic transformation. North Korea at that time lost the option of external balancing, namely alliances, so it devoted all its strength to internal balancing, through armaments, in order to deal with the collapse of the balance of power on the Korean Peninsula. Thus, South Korea may be open to negotiating an arrangement in which China, with US assent, secures the current North Korean regime. Considering Sino-US or Sino–South Korea relations, it is not realistic to expect that China could provide extended deterrence to North Korea, but the improvement of Sino–North Korea security ties may be a great help in easing the fears that North Korea has, and also matches the strategic interests of China. South Korea may consider this option if it helps North Korea to give up its nuclear weapons program because on balance South Korea's security would arguably increase under this circumstance.

IN SEARCH OF REGIONAL COOPERATION

What would be the best way to get the region to cooperate in solving the North Korea problem? And what is most likely to happen? I recommend a long-term plan to get the region to cooperate in solving the North Korea problem fundamentally, not just to resolve the North Korea nuclear issue.[14] For North Korea, the nuclear issue is deeply connected to the future of the regime and the stability of its rule. Dealing with this problem requires more than naïve engagement, hard-line punishment or the strategy of benign neglect. The "Sunshine" engagement policy pursued by Presidents Kim Dae Jung and Roh Moo Hyun, which offered unconditional support, failed to provide incentives for deep and permanent change in North Korea. On the other hand, coercive hard-line punishment, or a strategy of benign neglect only harden Pyongyang's perception of Seoul as an adversary rather than a partner. In fact, if the North Korean regime is pushed into a corner, it may become more risk-acceptant and choose to lash out to avoid a loss of face for the regime.[15] This situation would be very similar to the desperate mindset of "double or nothing" by terrorists who resort to suicide bombing, believing that they have nothing to lose. Nobody in the region wants to see such a worst-case scenario realized on the Korean Peninsula.

Thus, I recommend that the international society needs to provide North Korea with a face-saving exit even in a deep crisis and to persuade the North to accept the exit plan. In fact, there is a precedent for Pyongyang changing its course of action to save face. During the first nuclear crisis through the early 1990s, North Korea had confronted the United States but in June 1994 was suddenly willing to accommodate US demands in the face of the extreme danger to regime survival implied by UN sanctions and a prospective US attack.[16] This historical example shows that it is possible to narrow the reference points between North Korea and international society, and that coercion alone without a face-saving plan will probably make North Korea more risk-acceptant. In short, it is necessary for the region to find a way of getting North Korea to concede and change its course of action with its pride intact and without feeling disregarded.

NOTES

1. For the influence of China's rise on the Korean Peninsula in general, see Scott Snyder, *China's Rise and the Two Koreas: Politics, Economics, Security* (Boulder: Lynne-Rienner Publishers, 2009).

2. Robert O. Keohane and Joseph S. Nye Jr., *Power and Interdependence: World Politics in Transition* (Boston: Little Brown, 1977).

3. North Korea's decreasing dependence on South Korea is partially a result of China's economic rise but mainly due to the South Korean government's hard-line policy toward North Korea.

4. Compare 439.7 billion Korean won in 2007, the last year of Roh Moo Hyun government, with 14.1 billion Korean won in 2012, the last year of Lee Myung Bak government.

5. Office of the Secretary of Defense, Military and Security Developments Involving the People's Republic of China 2013, Annual Report to Congress (2013). See also Roger Cliff, Mark Burles, Michael S. Chase, Derek Eaton, Kevin L. Pollpeter, *Entering the Dragon's Lair: Chinese Antiaccess Strategies and Their Implications for the United States* (Santa Monica: RAND Corporation, 2007).

6. Jihwan Hwang, "The Two Koreas after U.S. Unipolarity: In Search of a New North Korea Policy," *Journal of International and Area Studies* 20, no. 1 (2013).

7. Chung-In Moon, *The Sunshine Policy: In Defense of Engagement as a Path to Peace in Korea* (Seoul: Yonsei University Press, 2012).

8. Most socio-economic reform programs can start with a new leadership. It does not mean a regime change but the change in the nature of leadership. For example, see the cases of reform program in Soviet Union under Mikhail S. Gorbachev and China under Mao Zedong. It is interesting to see how Myanmar pursues its reform program under a new leadership of President Thein Sein since 2011.

9. In this regards, the North Korean leadership sets a reference point in its internal and external policy and seeks not to lose face. For the North Korean leadership's reference point and face-saving, see Jihwan Hwang, "Face-Saving, Reference Point and North Korea's Strategic Assessments," *Korean Journal of International Studies* 49, no. 5 (2009).

10. Jihwan Hwang, "Getting Out of the Military-First Dilemmas: In Search of North Korea's Coevolution Military Strategy," EAI Asia Security Initiative Working Paper No. 17 (Seoul: East Asia Institute, 2011).

11. Chaesung Chun, "Moving from a North Korean Nuclear Problem to the Problem of North Korea," EAI Issue Briefing No. MASI #2009-03 (Seoul: East Asia Institute, 1 June 2009).

12. Hwang, "The Two Koreas."

13. Hillary Rodham Clinton, "America's Pacific Century," remarks at the East-West Center, Honolulu, Hawaii, 10 November 2011.

14. Chun, "Moving."

15. Hwang, "Face-Saving."

16. Joel S. Wit, Daniel B. Poneman, and Robert L. Gallucci, *Going Critical: The First North Korean Nuclear Crisis* (Washington, DC: Brookings Institution, 2004), 398. See also Don Oberdorfer, *The Two Koreas: A Contemporary History*, new ed. (New York: Basic Books, 2001).

CHAPTER 7

The North Korea Problem and China

Interests, Debates, and Roadmaps

ZHENG Jiyong

China sees the Korean Peninsula as its strategic frontier. During China's history, some of the largest-scale military operations have occurred on the Korean Peninsula. The latest campaign was the Korean War in the 1950s, through which China escaped from the possibility of control by the Soviet Union and the United States, and then leaped to the status of a major Asia-Pacific power.[1]

Korean affairs continue to be important to China's national interests.[2] The challenge is to discern the "core" interests within China's publicly-stated policy positions related to Korea. A close evaluation of these interests is warranted. Regarding both the short-term issues of the nuclear weapons crisis and provocation, as well as the longer-term issue of how North Korea fits into the region, do they really affect China's interests?

NATIONAL INTERESTS OF CHINA

The most significant characteristic of international relations on the Korean Peninsula is that the great powers pass the resolutions and the weak powers make the decisions.[3] The stability of relations among great powers brings the stability of the Korean Peninsula. From a structural point of view, the strategic interactions between China and the United States determine China's diplomatic policies toward the two Koreas, and those policies both reflect and impact Sino-US relations.[4] If Sino-US relations are relatively stable, relevant nations can basically ensure smooth North Korea nuclear crisis management. In Northeast Asia, if there is to be a soft landing for any crisis in the Korean Peninsula, great power coordination or compromise must be achieved.[5]

The main diplomatic strategies of the incumbent Chinese government can be summarized as "the big country is a valve key, the periphery is paramount, the developing countries are ground work, and multilateralism is an important stage."[6] The reality and history of the Korean Peninsula is the best example that can reflect China's diplomatic strategies. Since Xi Jinping took over the decision-making responsibility regarding foreign affairs, China's Korean Peninsula policy has shown a willingness to take proactive measures.[7] The process of solving the Korea problem has become a testing ground and a cornerstone for China to practice the new type of relationship between major countries.

Peace, stability, and denuclearization have always defined China's national interests on the Korean Peninsula. More concretely, we can say that actions that meet those three principles coincide with China's national interests, while opposite actions threaten China's interests.

In the short term, factors causing instability in the Korean Peninsula, especially the rapid development of nuclear issues, the instability of North Korea's politics (such as the execution of Jang Song Taek, raising concerns of instability in North Korea), and the uncertainty in the inter-Korea relationship, have affected China's interests. Since 2006, North Korea has conducted three nuclear tests, shocking the neighboring countries, including China, after which the sinking of the South Korean warship *Cheonan* and the Yeonpyeong Island incident also occurred.

On the North Korea nuclear crisis, China provides a clear and firm viewpoint in opposition to a nuclear DPRK. Firstly, the testing and development of nuclear weapons is threatening to China's national security. China does not want the number of its neighbors that possess nuclear weapons to increase. No country wants its neighbors to own nuclear weapons, no matter if it is a friend or an adversary, and this is the most basic principle of realism. At the same time, if it is true that "North Korea wants to sell its mature nuclear technologies to gain economic support,"[8] this nuclear proliferation will threaten China's security. In addition, North Korea's political instability can cause loss of control of nuclear technology or materials.

Secondly, North Korea's nuclear tests are greatly harmful to China's environmental safety. China has concerns about nuclear safety. The hazard of the Chernobyl accident is well known, and the leakage of the Japanese Fukushima nuclear plant has still not been controlled effectively. Since great powers such as the Soviet Union and Japan could not handle nuclear disasters effectively, it would be an environmental disaster for China if those nuclear problems occur in a relatively less developed country like North Korea. Earthquakes in China's frontier regions such as Yanbian were reported after the nuclear tests in 2009 and 2013, along with perceived tremors. The residents are not only afraid of the earthquakes, but also the health effects of nuclear radiation. Similarly, the Changbai (Paektu) Mountain is a dormant volcano, and nuclear tests may induce volcanic eruptions and earthquakes. If the Changbai Mountain were to erupt, a large area of China would suffer.

Thirdly, North Korea's possession of nuclear weapons may cause a domino effect, pushing Japan, Korea, and other countries, perhaps even Taiwan, to consider developing nuclear weapons. Although North Korea's possession of nuclear weapons is not the only reason for Japan and the ROK to pursue nuclear weapons, and sometimes just an excuse, it is indeed an incentive. Many politicians from the ROK have proposed developing and deploying nuclear weapons to deter North Korea.[9]

Fourthly, North Korea's possession of nuclear weapons will threaten China's international moral standing. As a founding member of the UN, a member of the International Atomic Energy Agency (IAEA), and a Member State of the Non-Proliferation Treaty (NPT), China bears much responsibility for global nuclear security and local stability. If it appears to be not playing a responsible role regarding the nuclear situation on the Korean Peninsula, China's international image as a responsible great power will be greatly damaged.

Furthermore, if there is a conflict between North Korea and the ROK, as the largest neighbor, China will not and cannot stay out. It is China's geo-political fate to be involved in Korean Peninsula affairs. The basic principles of China's policies toward the Korean Peninsula, such as a peace, stability, and denuclearization, can be understood logically. Therefore, China opposes the right of any party to threaten others, for those actions will result in an unstable situation. Although the Cold War ended long ago, the Cold War structure on the Korean Peninsula still remains, determined by geopolitics. Conflicts and instability on the Korean Peninsula will inevitably lead to a greater surrounding military presence and the expansion of armaments. Incidents such as *Cheonan* and Yeonpyeong Island, although they are not directly related to China, encouraged the United States, Japan, and the ROK to conduct military exercises on China's periphery frequently, which threatened China's security directly.[10]

In the long-term perspective, peace, stability, and denuclearization of the Korean Peninsula coincide with China's most important national interests. The core problem is the North Korea problem, namely how to make the DPRK integrate into the international community. China's starting-point is not to reconstruct or change North Korea. The reconstruction of its political trajectory will only bring internal instability, which will then lead to disorder and instability. North Korea is taking the *urisik* ("our style") path, which is different from the approaches taken by the ROK, Japan, and China, and we should respect the choice of their government. History has proven that a path that is not suitable for their actual situation will only bring chaos and instability. What China can do is to show to North Korea which path may be the most suitable one, for raising the quality of Korean people's livelihood, rather than forcing it to change.

As ROK President Park Geun-hye said, the lack of mutual trust, confidence, and international credibility has contributed to bad images on all sides. Mutual trust comes from confidence and international credibility. North Korea's top concern is regime security. After the former Soviet Union and Eastern European countries collapsed in the 1980s, and the establishment of diplomatic relations between Beijing and Seoul and between Seoul and Moscow, Pyongyang failed to get recognition from the United States and Japan in the mid-1990s. After that the relationship between Beijing and Pyongyang suffered from a long-term chill. Coupled with the effect of the recent Libya, Iraq, and Syria situations (even though these states abandoned the nuclear weapons or had no chemical weapons, their governments were condemned or attacked), North Korea's basic thesis that the great powers' promises are not credible, and that the dismantling of nuclear weapons and abandonment of other weapons will certainly lead to death, North Korea has been suffering from multilateral isolation. North Korea believes that only the possession of nuclear weapons can protect their regime and qualify them to negotiate with the United States. Therefore North Korea has advanced further and further along the path of developing missiles and nuclear weapons.

The beginning of a solution to this problem still lies in confidence, trust, and international credibility, especially between the DPRK and the United States. Since Pyongyang regards nuclear weapons as a panacea, we should try to make the DPRK government believe that nuclear weapons are useless to solve its basic problems—these weapons will not lead to prosperity, enhance Pyongyang's political self-confidence, increase the country's military security, or bring international prestige to North Korea.

Fortunately, North Korea is aware of this problem, is undergoing a positive change after the accession of Kim Jong Un, and is developing basically stably and in a relatively secure fashion. Currently, North Korea is gradually diluting its strong military focus, maintaining an appropriate conventional force, focusing on greater professionalism in its military, and withdrawing the influence of the military from economic fields; a number of young cadres who understand the economy and management are beginning to emerge on the political scene.[11]

Currently, North Korea is faced with several key issues. The first is to maintain political stability to make sure Kim Jong Un's government becomes more stable and more powerful. After a series of purges, the new regime led by Kim Jong Un has found a good solution to this problem. The second is to improve people's livelihood and economy. Long-term domestic and international political pressures had made livelihood issues stay in a secondary position, and so the military-first policy made the military services develop abnormally. What Kim Jong Un must do to solve this is to implement the provision of food and clothing to the people more effectively, as the public's expectations for the economy have become critical, and livelihood issues should be solved without delay.[12] Thirdly, people's support of the Rodong-dang (the Workers' Party) is still a problem. North Korea is faced with an unprecedented expansion of information flow, with more than a thousand markets (including underground markets) and more than 2.2 million mobile phones, information flow has shown explosive growth.[13] In this case, there will clearly be tension between faith in the leaders and the needs of the real world; how to solve this problem in order to maintain the Rodongdang's legitimacy is a serious topic.

Progress on peace on the Korean Peninsula runs in parallel with North Korea's integration into the international community. China hopes the Korean Peninsula can eventually achieve reunification under the premise of peace. China has confidence that even after the peaceful reunification of the Korean Peninsula, and even with the continued presence of US troops in the ROK, a unified Korean Peninsula will still be able to maintain friendly relations with China, just as has happened through history. From a practical point of view, US troops are also stationed in Japan, which makes China uneasy, but Japan has still maintained friendly relations with China for a long time.

THE DEBATE ABOUT HOW TO DEAL WITH NORTH KOREA

Needless to say, internal controversy, and sometimes very serious differences, exists in China on the problem of dealing with North Korea. In 2012 and 2013, this debate was particularly intense; even such issues as the abandonment of North Korea have become a public topic. Overall, the focus of this debate is how to position Sino–North Korea relations in the new era.

Is North Korea a geopolitical strategic asset or a burden to China? Traditional realists believe that North Korea retains usefulness as China's geopolitical barrier.[14] As in the Korean War, North Korea is still a springboard for maritime powers to invade the continental countries. As the security of North Korea and China are interdependent and indivisible, to protect North Korea is to defend China. Other realists believe that China has developed into a regional power, and even a global power, and although the Korean Peninsula cannot be regarded as the geopolitical barrier of Cold War era, it still plays an important role to consolidate and maintain China's position in Northeast Asia and East Asia. China should not abrogate its formal alliance with North Korea. It would be better for China to better take advantage of the potential value of the relationship with North Korea based on the reality of Northeast Asia. Some liberals say, however, that China should not keep the traditional conservative notion of realism regarding the value of North Korea and the Korean Peninsula any longer because China's geopolitical boundaries are far beyond the Korean Peninsula and Northeast Asia, so China can compete with the United States at the global level. While North Korea's actions have become a serious burden and drag for the expansion of the frontiers of China's interests, insisting on traditional China-DPRK relations will be harmful to China and Northeast Asia. Therefore China and North Korea should either return to normal relations, or China should abandon North Korea.[15]

Should China still cling to North Korea, or favor the ROK instead? One view is that North Korea remains the key to solve the problems of Northeast Asia, and it stands at the most disadvantaged position of all the parties. Although the global structure of the Cold War no longer exists, the Korean Peninsula is still a living fossil of the Cold War, and the traditional geopolitical concepts and recognitions still function. The ROK and the United States have a traditional military alliance relationship and both of them still do not trust China on the issues of politics and security, so China should take into account the concerns and needs of North Korea.[16] Another point of view holds that the Korean Peninsula has fundamentally changed, and the fact that the ROK and China established diplomatic ties twenty years ago proves that the ROK is not a real threat to China; the real threat to China's security is North Korea's perverse and eccentric behavior, as it constantly creates incidents that force China to expend its limited foreign affairs resources, making China waste too much energy on the Korean Peninsula. China should give more consideration to the ROK, whose behavior is more normal, not North Korea. The third view is that China is already a world-level political and military power, and the Korean Peninsula issue should be considered on the basis of the broad framework of Sino-US relations, taking into account the balance of the ROK and North Korea. Hence the economic policies should be more inclined to North Korea, to influence the future development of North Korea, and the political and security policies more inclined to the ROK, to include it in China's sphere of influence to a greater extent.[17]

Does a reunified Korean Peninsula conform to China's national interests? There are two kinds of controversy about this issue. From a realist perspective, the reunified Korea will be a medium-sized country with nearly eighty million people, and China is uncertain whether it would be *pro*-China or *anti*-China. Therefore, compared with this uncertainty, the current situation is somewhat under control. Meanwhile, the reunified Korea would not only possess nuclear weapons, but may also put forward claims on the territory of China. Therefore, China does not want to face a unified Korea. Furthermore, China is concerned about the possible stationing of US troops in Korea after unification. South Korea has proposed a variety of paths, but these do not include withdrawing US troops from the Korean Peninsula. For hundreds of years, China's goal has been to prevent hostile forces from coming close to its border and has concentrated its attention, over the centuries, on the Korean Peninsula. There have been several large-scale wars for the Korean Peninsula.[18] A second point of view is that, historically, China's prosperity is tied to the Korean Peninsula's prosperity and China does not have to worry about the reunification of the Korean Peninsula. On the contrary, China could benefit from a unified Korean market.

The following issues reflect these arguments, which also reflect the understanding of the Korean Peninsula issue among Chinese academics. First is the understanding of the DPRK regime. China and North Korea are both socialist countries and face the profound historical challenge of economically developing within a capitalist global system. At present, North Korea and China have the same political aims. Supporting such a socialist country is China's duty and obligation, and is evidence of the legitimacy of the Chinese system. Others believe that China's pursuit of stability and peace should be based on the overall situation: the whole Korean Peninsula region, rather than just the North Korea regime.

Second is the understanding of nuclear issues. There are different interpretations of nuclear weapons, nuclear research, and nuclear proliferation. Some people support the ideas of the United States and South Korea, who insist that North Korea must stop all nuclear activities, including research and development. Others argue that the nuclear issue has historical roots. The perceived security threat from the United States and South Korea and the lack of international nuclear morals led to North Korea possessing nuclear weapons. Therefore, the issue of nuclear disarmament should be carried out step by step. Accordingly, some people believe that China should maximize the use of the North Korea nuclear issue to confront the United States and Japan's militarism. North Korea should consider eliminating its nuclear weapons only after obtaining concessions from its adversaries.

Third is the understanding of the relationship between DPRK policy and overall security in Northeast Asia. Some people insist that North Korea's behavior led to the deterioration of the regional security environment through nuclear and missile development, provocative behavior, and unwillingness to make peace with Seoul. Others insist that the instability is coming from the United States.

Fourth is that China should persuade or tame North Korea through specific methods of operation, which raises the question of whether China actually has the capability to control Korea. Some people have the idea that China has absolute control over North Korea, including in the areas of security, economy, and ideology, but China is reluctant to use and exert such influence and control. Another argument is that China and North Korea only have a close relationship on the surface.[19]

A CHINA-STYLE LOGIC FOR PROBLEM SOLVING AND A ROADMAP

China has its own logic for problem solving. The Korean Peninsula issue is essentially a development issue. With economic growth and improvement in people's livelihood, the Korean Peninsula would not fall into a security dilemma.

Although there are debates within China on how to deal with the Korean Peninsula issue, peace, stability, and denuclearization are the three basic principles that encompass China's national interests. China believes that approaches undertaken thus far by the United States cannot resolve the Korean Peninsula crisis.

China should become a supplier of public goods in Northeast Asia by creating and providing norms for regional peace and stability.[20] On security, China's goal is for cooperative security and reasonable safety. Economically, China should focus on economic integration in Northeast Asia. North Korea can restore its confidence and find new economic growth with the help of Japan and South Korea based on the principle of economic integration.

Culturally, China should focus on reunification in the future. Most importantly, the relationship between South and North Korea should be considered as a special state-to-state relationship, premised on the idea that Korea is a divided nation that will eventually be reunified. Additionally, East Asian countries should recognize the value of China's approach that is relatively comprehensive. At the operational level, China has insisted on an economic, cultural, and military three-pronged strategy. For a long time, the United States promoted a Northeast Asia strategy based on the US-ROK alliance and the US-Japan alliance, while attempting to ensure absolute security through military power. But this kind of security-oriented strategic logic has reached a dead end.[21] China should promote a new path. At present, there is rapid growth in economic cooperation between China and South Korea. South Korea is proposing to deepen cultural exchanges with China to enhance mutual political trust. Sino-ROK security cooperation has also been showing a rapid development momentum.[22]

In consultation with other countries, the following national interests must be protected. It is essential that Korea's role as China's strategic frontier should not disappear. China will not tolerate unrest and conflict in the areas surrounding China. North Korea's internal and external stability and development must be guaranteed. Also, in relation to Korean Peninsula affairs, China's status as the most important neighbor and that of other relevant actors should not be changed. In some respects, China's dominant status in Korean Peninsula affairs should not be neglected or abandoned. Finally, geographically, the presence of foreign forces should not disrupt Chinese psychological boundaries. For centuries, China has been striving to reject foreign intervention in the Korean Peninsula. In 1950, China suffered massive casualties when it sent troops into the Korean Peninsula to fight against the US forces. The reason is that the decision makers at the time believed that if the US military passed the 38th parallel, it would be tantamount to a violation of China's sovereignty.[23]

So, China's fundamental principles cannot be compromised. These issues can be listed as follows: First, North Korea has nuclear weapons, but China's determination to denuclearize North Korea is unchangeable. North Korea's possession of nuclear weapons will not only threaten China's national security, but also be a challenge to regional and international order, especially to China's authority, and may lead to a regional nuclear arms race. Second,

North Korea has the right to choose its own road, which must be respected. So far, the national condition of Pyongyang is caused by its form of government. The form of the government should not be changed by external force; it can only be improved during the process of development instead of being overturned. Third, provocative words and deeds are not helpful. Continuing to stir up trouble will be a threat not only to the Korean Peninsula, but also to its surrounding countries. The Korean Peninsula is the gateway to China.

With consultation and persuasion, compromises may be made on some secondary issues. Firstly is the development path of North Korea: North Korea tries to develop its military power and deterrence due to its severe security anxiety. China should actively promote dialogue and urge all sides to create a good surrounding environment to encourage North Korea so that it will dismantle its nuclear weapons. By developing and promoting its political confidence, North Korea will realize that only development, not nuclear weapons, can maintain its security.[24] Secondly is the pattern of reunification: China has never opposed the reunification of the Korean Peninsula, regardless of whether it would be under a federal system or a confederal system, or tried to make the two Koreas wait for reunification. As long as the process is peaceful, Pyongyang and Seoul can make their own decisions, including the future of the United States Forces Korea (USFK). Thirdly is the way to solve the dispute: Under the principle of consultation, the dispute can be solved by negotiation without threatening, intimidation, blackmailing, or brinksmanship.[25]

To come to an agreement, China will possibly make compromises with surrounding countries in the following aspects. Initially, faced with our common security problems in Northeast Asia, China should take regional interests into consideration to cooperate with surrounding countries on the nuclear issue. Additionally, during the execution of the agreement, China can also make compromises. For example, China supports the implementation of the 9.19 Agreement and UN resolutions, which contain many bilateral agreements that may be helpful for it to promote international trust and nurture its superpower identity. And lastly, China can make practical compromises in the implementation of the principle of not threatening the peace and stability of Northeast Asia.[26]

In China's view, a roadmap to peace should include four processes: the construction of confidence and trust, integration of North Korea into international society, denuclearization of North Korea, and achieving stability and peace.[27] First of all, the minimum goal is to develop the confidence that North Korea can achieve stability and peace. Without other countries' interference and with support from the outside, North Korea and South Korea should try their best to trust each other. Second, the mid-term goal is to reach an agreement on the future of the Korean Peninsula, which means deciding under what conditions all sides can coexist and promote common development. A country outside the international society cannot drive its regional development. So, during this period, to achieve the goal that North Korea can be integrated into the region and into the international society, relevant countries can play a role to support and supervise its denuclearization and political and national development. Finally, South Korea and North Korea can achieve unification via pragmatic means and bilateral agreements.

NOTES

1. Shen Zhihua, *Mao Zedong, Stalin and the Korean War* (Guangzhou: Guangdong People's Press, 2003), 116.

2. Li Xiguang, "DPRK is China's first level core interest" [in Korean], *Gongshiwang*, accessed 20 July 2014, http://www.21ccom.net/articles/qqsw/zlwj/article
    _2010120125541.html.

3. Bai Jie, *Notes of Observing the Korean Peninsula* (World Knowledge Press: Beijing, 2013), 261.

4. Wang Yisheng, *The Management of the Korean Peninsula Conflicts* (Military Science Press: Beijing, 2011), 52.

5. Bai Jie, *Notes of Observing*, 264.

6. Zheng Jiyong, "China's Perspectives and Strategies towards the Korean Peninsula Peace Regime," paper presented at the meeting on the Project for Korean Foreign Affairs, Shanghai, China, 5 December 2013.

7. Institute for Far Eastern Studies, *The Korean Peninsula: 2013 Evaluation and 2014 Prospects* (Seoul: Institute for Far Eastern Studies, Kyungnam University, 2013), 75–92.

8. Hong Nack Kim, "China's Policy toward North Korea under the Xi Jinping Leadership," *North Korean Review* 9, no. 2 (2013): 83–98.

9. Ted Galen Carpenter, "South Korea's Growing Nuclear Flirtation," 25 April 2013, *RealClearPolitics.com*, http://www.realclearpolitics.com/articles /2013/04/25/south_koreas_growing_nuclear_flirtation_118132.html.

10. Zheng Jiyong, "The 'Conflict-Reconciliation' Cycle on the Korean Peninsula: A Chinese Perspective," *Korean Journal of Defense Analysis* 24, no. 1 (Spring 2012): 123–39.

11. Zhao Huji, "China's Perspectives and Strategies towards North Korea Development Cooperation," paper presented at the meeting for the International Cooperation for Enhancing Peace in North East Asia and North Korea's Development, Seoul, 19 November 2013.

12. Pyongyang has stipulated the "parallel promotion" of economic growth and nuclear armament in its constitution.

13. Kim Sangbae, "Roles of Middle Power in East Asia: A Korean Perspective," paper presented at conference on The Role of Middle Power in the 21st Century International Relations, KAIS-KF International Conference, 19–20 April 2013, Seoul.

14. Yoon Daekyu, *Inconvenient Truth on North Korea* (Hanul Academy: Seoul, 2013), 47.

15. Deng Yuwen, "China Should Abandon North Korea," *Financial Times*, 27 February 2013, http://www.ft.com/cms/s/0/9e2f68b2-7c5c-11e2-99f0 -00144feabdc0.html.

16. Wang Chuanjian, *Double Regulation: America's Korean Peninsula Policy after the Cold War* (World Knowledge Press: Beijing, 2003).

17. Deng Yuwen, "China Should Abandon North Korea."

18. Zhao Huji, "China's Perspectives and Strategies."

19. Shim Jae Hoon, "North Korea Tests China and the World," *Yale Global*, 28 January 2013, http://yaleglobal.yale.edu/content/north-korea-tests-china -and-world.

20. Oliver Stuenkel, "Who Will Make the Rules in Tomorrow's World?" *Post Western World*, 24 November 2012, http://www.postwesternworld.com /2012/11/24/who-will-makes-the-rules-in-tomorrows-world/.

21. Zheng Jiyong, "Chinese Perspective on Regional Implications of the NPT," in *Developing A Region: Sketching A Path Towards Harmony* (Jeju, Korea: Friedrich Naumann Stiftung and Jeju Peace Institute, 2010), 154–63.

22. Zheng Jiyong, "China's Perspectives and Strategies towards the Korean Peninsula Peace regime," paper presented at the meeting for the Project for Korea Foreign Affairs, Shanghai, 5 December 2013.

23. English.news.cn, "Chinese FM, U.N. Chief Discuss the Korean Peninsula Tensions," 6 April 2013, http://news.xinhuanet.com/english/china/2013 -04/06/c_132288307.htm.

24. Wang Hong Guang, "If North Korea's Nuclear Facilities Suffer an Attack by the United States and South Korea, the Nuclear Pollution Will Be A Disaster for China" [in Korean], *Huanqiu Shibao* (Global Times), 16 December 2013, http://mil.huanqiu.com/observation/2013-12/4665829 .html.

25. Zheng, "China's Perspectives and Strategies."

26. Jae Seongho, "Armistice Agreement under Korean Security Environment and Future Peace Management Regime" [in Korean], *Gukbang Jeong Chaek Yeongu* 100 (2013): 9.

27. Zheng, "The 'Conflict-Reconciliation' Cycle."

CHAPTER 8

Explaining Japan's North Korea Policy

Yoichiro SATO

Japan's Asia policy during the Cold War period was largely shaped by the regional Cold War framework, most importantly the alliance with the United States. Japan was to support the Republic of Korea (South Korea) on the divided Korean Peninsula. However, Japan's physical and social proximity to Asia required it to attempt to carve out some diplomatic space in its dealings with communist Asia.[1] Japan's ambivalent approach toward North Korea has persisted into the post–Cold War period.

Japan's policy toward North Korea has also been a reverse image of Japan's relations with South Korea. Having difficulties with South Korea's politicization of the colonial history, Japan has used its limited relations with North Korea not to the extent of "balancing" its relations with South Korea, but reminding the South Koreans of its displeasure. The North-South reconciliation during two successive South Korea governments (1999–2009) opened a possibility for Japan to develop a closer relationship with both, but the increasing security concerns about the North have dissuaded Japan from a rapid reconciliation.

Social linkages with North Korea further complicate Japan's foreign policy toward North Korea. The issues of Japanese citizens trapped in North Korea (spouses of the repatriated Koreans and the abductees) and North Korea hosting the Japanese Red Army terrorists continue to be both a reason for and an obstacle to bilateral communication.

The geographical proximity and social linkage have not made Japan a key player in the regional diplomacy over North Korea. Japan's relevance is viewed as peripheral at best[2] and distractive at worst[3] in the multilateral diplomacy over the nuclear crisis. However, in the long-term regional geopolitical context, Japan and its policy deriving from the ongoing North Korea crisis have been cast in a more important regard.[4] Most importantly, the ongoing crises have shaped the course of the US-Japan alliance review.[5]

In this chapter, I will attempt to explain Japan's convergence with and divergence from the United States and South Korea in their policies toward North Korea, focusing on Japan's alliance with the United States, relations with South Korea, and domestic politics. During the post–Cold War years, Japan's divergence has from time to time shifted toward the tougher end, compared to its allies, but it has also sought dialogues with the North when its allies did not. Why?

BACKGROUND

Japan relinquished its colonial sovereignty over the Korean Peninsula by signing the San Francisco Peace Treaty in 1951. The intensifying confrontation between the capitalist United States and the communist Soviet Union and the People's Republic of China (PRC) had recast the Korean Peninsula into a new geopolitical rivalry, with each camp respectively supporting its client regime. When a war broke out between the North and the South Korean regimes in June 1950, the disarmed Japan did not become an active and direct participant (with some exceptions).[6] The US military bases throughout Japan quickly became the launching pads of the US war operations, and this emergency arrangement was endorsed in a new mutual security treaty in 1951. Japan and South Korea normalized their relations in 1965, while Japan did not seek official diplomatic relations with North Korea.

Although Japan has not opened diplomatic representation in North Korea to this date, informal relations with North Korea have been cultivated and sustained throughout the post–Korean War period. Most Korean residents who came to Japan before and during the war sought repatriations to their homes in North and South, while some stayed as naturalized Japanese citizens or as "special permanent residents." The North Korea government, through its closely affiliated agents in the General Association of Korean Residents in Japan, or Chongryon, actively recruited returnees from Japan with the promise of a communist paradise. The estimated 93,000 people who repatriated to North Korea under the Chongryon program since 1959 included an estimated 6,000 Japanese spouses and an unknown number of their children.[7] In reality, the kinship ties with Japan became an important lifeline for North Korea's fledgling economy. Many Japanese spouses (mostly female) in North Korea were trapped there, and Japan's government came under pressure to seek their return.

Terrorism provided another reason for continuing communication with North Korea. A group of Japanese Red Army hijackers seized an airliner in 1970 and ordered the pilots to head to Pyongyang after releasing passengers at Fukuoka and Seoul. Japan has tried to obtain information about these terrorists and facilitate their repatriations as criminal suspects. While their children were granted Japanese citizenships and repatriated, the remaining Red Army members in 2004 requested their return to Japan as asylum seekers as opposed to criminal hijackers.[8]

Furthermore, mysterious disappearances of Japanese citizens on the Sea of Japan and other coasts and in Europe in the late 1970s to early 1980s raised suspicion of abductions. While Japan looked for these "specially designated missing persons" without naming North Korea as the culprit until much later, such suspicion was growing.

THE US ALLIANCE AS A FACTOR

Although Japan, as an ally of the United States, mostly toes the latter's regional security policy line, occasional divergences are common. Japan's geographical proximity to and increasing economic interdependence with China have worked in both advocating moderation in US regional security policy and urging stronger US commitment to regional security. As US-China relations have had ups and downs, Japan's stance toward China has not been in perfect synchronization with the United States, and the resulting divergence has affected Japan's policy toward North Korea as well.

Japan has been ambivalent about China's diplomatic role toward North Korea. At the outset of the nuclear crisis in the early 1990s, US bilateral dealing with North Korea left little room for inputs by Japan. Japan grudgingly stayed behind US President Bill Clinton's bilateral negotiation (through his special envoy former president Jimmy Carter), after lodging its opposition to military actions against North Korea at the time.[9] Japan was not satisfied with two aspects of the outcome of the bilateral negotiation—assigning to Japan a large part of the light-water reactors construction in North Korea and not addressing North Korea's ballistic missiles whose range had already covered the western half of Japan at the time.[10]

Behind the United States' deal with North Korea was an optimism that North Korea's regime would collapse soon.[11] Japan was more cautious and also ambivalent about such an outcome, for instability in North Korea would most directly affect proximate countries including Japan. North Korea had violated a series of international agreements and later UN resolutions to refrain from launching ballistic missiles. North Korea's test launching of a long-range Taepodong missile in 1998 nearly caused Japan to withdraw from funding of the light-water reactors, but the United States and others persuaded Japan to stay within the agreed framework. Japan demanded that the United States negotiate a freeze on North Korea's ballistic missile program. Secretary of State Madeline Albright's visit to Pyongyang, however, only produced a North Korea agreement to "indefinitely postpone" launching of long-range ballistic missiles—ambiguous language to be abused by North Korea in the following years.[12] The 1998 missile test became a major catalyst for Japan to overcome domestic opposition against participation in joint research on Theater Missile Defense (TMD) with the United States. Consideration of China's verbal opposition to the TMD[13] yielded to the threat perception against North Korea, and Prime Minister Junichiro Koizumi in 2002 announced Japan's participation.

The shift in the US approach to the North Korea problems under the George W. Bush administration was a welcome development for Japan, but did not solve Japan's ambivalence. On one hand, the new Six-Party Talks (6PT) framework assured Japan a voice on the North Korea matters.

This was a relief for Japan, as it had struggled to be included in the face of South Korea's efforts to keep Japan out through most of the 1990s. On the other hand, US reliance on China's chairing of the 6PT reminded Japan of the Clinton-era "Japan passing" when the United States called China a "strategic partner." The use of the Trilateral Coordination and Oversight Group (TCOG) mechanism among the United States, Japan, and South Korea during the first term of the Bush administration was supposed to ease Japan's fear that the United States and China might be calling the shots. However, South Korea President Roh Moo Hyun's radically pro-North approach caused a major divergence from the other two countries, making the TCOG dysfunctional, and the United States in Bush's second term stopped using the TCOG mechanism under Assistant Secretary of State Christopher Hill. There also was a concern in the US government that Japan's abduction issue could become an obstacle in the overall negotiation. This fear was also a product of self-reflection among core members of the US negotiating team (such as the Secretary of State Condoleezza Rice, National Security Advisor Steve Hadley, and Christopher Hill), who saw others in the same government (such as Vice President Dick Cheney and President Bush) still wishing for a regime change. But, the major turn in the second Bush administration was that Bush saw opening, not isolation, of North Korea as the way to "regime change."[14] Japan has avoided being made a scapegoat for failed talks by staying in, despite a complete lack of progress on the abduction issue since 2004.

Japan's abduction issue is in a catch-22 situation. North Korea is willing to approach Japan only when it is completely isolated from the other members of the 6PT, and Japan must negotiate the abduction issue without rewarding North Korea outside the 6PT framework. US negotiators have frequently forgotten that they too were in multilateral talks. In response, while Japan did not completely spoil the talks, it did express its dissatisfaction via withholding of financial contributions to multilateral efforts. The pattern was repeated when the United States delisted North Korea from the list of terror sponsors (thereby lifting part of its financial sanctions against North Korea) in 2008 in exchange for agreeing with the United States to start the first step of dismantling the nuclear capabilities. The last gambit of President Bush cost the United States 400 million dollars in aid, but North Korea only demolished a cooling-water tower at the Yongbyon complex. Japan did not join the aid group and maintained its financial sanctions against North Korea.

The repeated nuclear tests (2006, 2009, and 2013) and missile tests by North Korea and its two major military provocations against South Korea in 2010 have suspended the 6PT, and these issues have been referred to the United Nations Security Council (UNSC). President Obama's call to negotiate with North Korea "anywhere, anytime" was conditioned by a firm US stance not to reward North Korea for merely appearing at meetings. As this US stance became clear toward the latter half of 2009, North Korea announced that it would not return to the 6PT. This development did not increase Japan's fear of US bilateralism. However, shifting of the center of negotiations to the UNSC increased the weight of China and Russia when negative (unlike the positives in the 6PT) inducements for North Korea were to be discussed. Japan was a nonpermanent member of UNSC, 2005–2006 and 2009–2010, and worked closely with the United States in preparing UNSC resolutions. In 2006, Japan played an important role in the preparations of two key resolutions. In response to North Korea's missile test in July 2006, Japan sponsored UNSC Resolution 1695, which denounced the test, demanded North Korea suspend its missile programs, abandon nuclear programs, and return to the 6PT and the IAEA framework of inspection.[15] Japan's call for sanctions under UN Charter 7, however, met threats of veto from China and Russia, and a resulting US effort to persuade it to settle on softer language. North Korea's defiance and a nuclear test three months later encouraged Japan to sponsor UNSC Resolution 1718, which incorporated the language of complete, verifiable, irreversible disarmament of North Korea and added sanctions under UN Charter 7 to empower the demands of the resolutions.[16] The UNSC Resolution 1874 in response to North Korea's third nuclear test in May 2009 enabled maritime forced inspection of cargo ships suspected of carrying WMD-related cargo.[17]

Although credits are due to various actors for the improved cooperation in the UN Security Council, the close and patient diplomatic coordination between the United States and Japan in 2006 and 2009 to work the international public opinion raised the diplomatic cost for China to continue behaving as North Korea's guardian and eventually cornered China into agreeing to sanctions against North Korea. The UNSC Resolution 1874 in 2009 and absence of US bilateral flirtation with North Korea since then have marked a limited success for Japanese diplomacy. However, given the experience of the failed 6PT in 2008, Japan is worrying about a similar misguided venture by Obama in his lame duck years.

SOUTH KOREA RELATIONS AS A FACTOR

Although Japan's official diplomatic tie on the Korean Peninsula is with South Korea only, both the government in Pyongyang and Japan have seen in each other a degree of utility as a diplomatic bargaining chip in conducting their respective relations with South Korea. Democratization of South Korea and the shift of its leadership from conservative military-affiliated presidents to civilian politicians have transformed the nature of anti-Japan themes in South Korea politics from a theatric performance into a tool of partisan attacks. The resulting discord in South Korea–Japan relations since the 1990s have tempted Japan to use its "North Korea card" at times.

The Sunshine policy of President Kim Dae Jung and its continuation through the Roh Moo Hyun government allowed Japan to approach North Korea in two regards. First, consideration of South Korea's policy of confrontation vis-à-vis the North was no longer needed. Quite to the contrary, it was Japan that remained skeptical of North Korea's intentions in approaching Seoul and the South's unsuspecting and emotional embrace of the North. Second (and in some contradiction to the first reasoning), Japan had to hedge against a real possibility that the North was actually opening up. Japan wanted to keep its foot in the North Korean market before competition between China and South Korea would dominate North Korea's economy. If diplomatic normalization with North Korea and payment of indemnity for colonial rule were inevitable eventualities, Japan had to carefully time its entry in order to recoup some of its own payment through mutually beneficial economic exchanges. Prime Minister Koizumi's second visit to Pyongyang in 2004 was to be followed by a planned delegation of general contractors within the same year ahead of the bilateral working-level normalization talks, but the visit was cancelled at the last minute.[18] Japan's payment of an indemnity and infrastructure development contracts have not materialized.

Prime Minister Koizumi's visit to the Yasukuni Shrine in April 2002 did not invite a strong reaction from President Kim Dae Jung in his final year of presidency, and in September Koizumi made his first visit to Pyongyang. The succeeding South Korea President Roh Moo Hyun welcomed a "future-oriented" relationship with Koizumi,[19] but the bilateral relationship soon deteriorated as Koizumi annualized his visits to Yasukuni during his five-year tenure. Japan's approach to North Korea under the deteriorating relationship with Seoul allowed the North to take more advantage of the liberal leadership in Seoul, while Japan pursued its domestic agenda of solving the abduction issue.

The US efforts to trilateralize its alliances with Japan and South Korea have been pursued by Victor Cha[20] (who became the Director for Asian Affairs in the National Security Council), among others, but had to wait for the end of Roh Moo Hyun's term as president. Despite the nuclear testing by North Korea in 2006, in the following year Roh told US Secretary of Defense Robert Gates that the United States and Japan were the greatest threats in Asia.[21] The lack of progress in North-South political relations led to South Korea's disillusionment with the Sunshine policy and, along with other factors, the election of the conservative government of Lee Myung Bak in late 2007. North Korea's increasing vigilance since it failed to meet the deadline to declare the complete nuclear accounting as agreed in the 6PT in 2008 drove Lee to pursue closer trilateral military cooperation against North Korea. More frequent joint military exercises resulted, in response to North Korea's sinking of a Korean naval corvette, the *Cheonan*, and shelling of the Yeonpyeong Island in 2010.[22] Unlike Roh, Lee advocated a strong response against North Korea's provocation, calling for retaliatory air and artillery strikes, of which only the latter was implemented as a result of US dissuasion.[23]

However, diplomatic rows between South Korea and Japan over the disputed island of Takeshima (Korean name: Dokdo) and the wartime "comfort women" issue resurfaced near the end of Lee Myung Bak's presidency. Suffering from declining public support and a corruption charge against a family member, and frustrated by Japanese Prime Minister Abe's refusal to discuss compensation for the comfort women, Lee landed on Takeshima in August 2012 as the first president to do so. As South Korea's new conservative president Park Geun-hye continued to employ her predecessor's anti-Japan rhetoric, Abe in May 2013 responded by dispatching his cabinet advisor, Isao Iijima (who also served Prime Minister Koizumi and played a key role in his visits to Pyongyang in 2002 and 2004), to Pyongyang.[24] Without any prospect of reopening the 6PT, Abe allowed North Korea to use the image of improving relations with Japan, presumably for some prospects of progress on the abduction issue. While the visit did not immediately lead to reopening of the bilateral talks on abduction, the *Asahi* newspaper on 28 January 2014 reported that three high-ranking Japanese diplomats were in Hanoi possibly to meet a North Korean counterpart—news the Japanese government quickly denied.[25] A series of secret and informal talks led to official resumption of the bilateral normalization talks in early 2014. Japan's conservatives are critical of Abe's approach to Pyongyang, thinking that North Korea has taken more advantage of Japan than the other way around.[26] As Park Geun-hye continues to play up the anti-Japanese agenda and confronts Abe's nationalist agenda (such as his visit to the Yasukuni Shrine in December 2013), talks with North Korea serve as Japan's diplomatic card vis-à-vis South Korea as well.

DOMESTIC POLITICS AS A FACTOR

The end of the Cold War opened up a path for more flexible North Korea policy by Japan at least for a few years before the North's development of nuclear weapons grew into a serious crisis toward 1994. During the final years of the Liberal Democratic Party's (LDP) uninterrupted reign over Japanese politics since 1955, however, the party failed to take diplomatic advantage of a weak North Korea. At the end of the Cold War, the Soviet aid to North Korea was disappearing, and the Chinese barter trade was shrinking as China demanded cash payments for its trade. The complete reversal of the power position vis-à-vis South Korea, and the South's diplomatic openings with both the Soviet Union and China isolated North Korea. The senior LDP faction leader Shin Kanemaru's visit to Pyongyang in late 1990 very well illustrated the lack of leadership in the Japanese government and its inability to conduct strategic diplomacy at the time of its advantage vis-à-vis North Korea. Kanemaru floated the opening of discussions with North Korea to start diplomatic relations, an idea Japan's diplomats stopped short of.[27] When Kanemaru was indicted of tax fraud and an undisclosed donation from a major domestic courier, the search of his house yielded hidden unauthenticated gold ingots, which were rumored to be attributable to the aid he had delivered to North Korea.[28] Japanese politicians at the time were merely using North Korea's opening to their personal advantage in the same manner they had profited from Japan's reparations to South Korea decades earlier or Japan's overseas development assistance elsewhere,[29] regardless of the growing US concerns about North Korea at a time when Japan's worthiness as an ally was being tested in the Persian Gulf War.

The abductee issue became a key feature of Japanese policy toward North Korea only after the nuclear weapons development by North Korea became a regional security concern. Some critical evidence had emerged near the end of the Cold War period, through the arrests of North Korean agents, Shin Gwang-su in 1985[30] and Kim Hyon Hui in 1987. In 1988, one of the abductees, Kaoru Matsuki, managed to send a letter to his family and named two other abductees who lived in Pyongyang. Given what Japanese leaders knew, Kanemaru's not raising the abduction issue during his Pyongyang visit in 1990 was deliberate.

The abduction issue became a bipartisan issue, attracting members into the League of Parliamentarians Concerned about the Abductions (Rachi Giren). However, lobbying by the members of the Rachi Giren backed by family members of the suspected abductees did not immediately force the government to approach North Korea throughout the 1990s when its compliance with the 1994 Geneva Agreed Framework was partial at best while it test-fired ballistic missiles with increasing ranges.

Prime Minister Koizumi's diplomatic gambit in September 2002 to visit Pyongyang and negotiate the return of abductees was carried out under South Korea President Kim Dae Jung's strong determination to cement friendship with North Korea through unilateral economic aid. The softening of South Korea's policy gave the Japanese government an opportunity to use its own positive inducement toward the North without agitating South Korea. Koizumi managed to bring back five abductees in 2002, but North

Korea declared that all of the rest had died. Koizumi visited Pyongyang again in 2004 and managed to arrange the return of five North Korea–born children and one American spouse of the abductees. The consecutive governments since 2006 have set a cabinet portfolio of the Minister in Charge of the Abduction Affairs. The timing of Koizumi's two visits, the first just before the United States was about to confront North Korea with an allegation of hiding a uranium-based nuclear weapons program, and the second after the North Korea negotiator walked out of a meeting with US Assistant Secretary of State Jim Kelly, risked openly diverging from US policy priorities. However, the two countries closely coordinated to minimize their policy divergence after 2002, allowing Japan just enough diplomatic maneuvering space to exploit a small window of opportunity to get some abductees' family members back without weakening their collective position on the nuclear issue.

Japan managed to include the abduction issue in the overall agenda of the 6PT, but in separate bilateral discussions with North Korea. When orchestrated pressure from China and the United States brought North Korea to the 6PT in 2005, Japan signed on to the overall agreement, which set in motion a step-by-step exchange of concessions by all sides toward nuclear disarmament of the North, despite lack of development on the abduction issue.[31] Japan, however, did not agree to any new financial assistance to the North except humanitarian aid. The Japanese governments after Koizumi have continuously pursued the abduction issue, but they had to carefully weigh the risk of taking the blame for overall negotiation failures at the 6PT. Japan doubted the sincerity of North Korea's brief return to the 6PT in 2008 after it conducted nuclear explosion tests in 2006. Japan was critical of the US decision to lift part of the financial sanctions on North Korea. However, general public interest in the abduction issue had lost the level of intensity compared to the 2002–2004 period.

In March 2009, the son of abducted Yaeko Taguchi visited South Korea and met Kim Hyon Hui, who told him that his mother was alive (despite North Korea's claim that she had died in 1986).[32] The news briefly invoked a renewed public interest in the abduction issue, but as Kim did not produce any tangible new evidence to back her belief about Taguchi, public interest in the abduction issue quickly waned. The abductees and their families today do not form a coherent lobbying group, but preference for negotiations over sanctions has grown after the leadership succession in North Korea to Kim Jong Un.[33]

Japan's resumption of the normalization talks with North Korea in early 2014 despite North Korea's long-range missile test in December 2012 and the third nuclear explosion test in February 2013 does not imply taking over of Japan's North Korea policy by the abduction lobby, but rather a return of strategic thinking and primacy of the Foreign Ministry in Japan's North Korea diplomacy under Abe.[34]

CONCLUSION

Japan's policy toward North Korea is first and foremost conducted within the framework of the US-Japan alliance, which focuses on rolling back North Korea's nuclear weapons development. However, a containment approach exclusively utilizing negative inducements would meet opposition from China. The US return to a mixed approach of positive and negative inducements during the second Bush administration ironically raised China's relative weight in regional diplomacy, thereby placing Japan in a competition against China for US attention.

South Korea's oscillations between hard and soft approaches toward the North have interacted with the periodic rises of anti-Japanese stances in its domestic politics. Japan has coped with these complex political dynamics by prioritizing its relations with the South over the North, while using the North as a reminder against the South's excessive anti-Japanese tilt.

The domestic politics of Japan have not only been responsible for Japan's hard-line policy against North Korea in relation to the abduction issue, but also for its soft policy. Anticipated payment of wartime reparations to North Korea has been linked with domestic pork-barreling. After 2004, however, both the abduction issue and the reparations issue on the normalization agenda have been subordinated to the nuclear and missile issues. As of late 2014, the fate of the ongoing bilateral consultations on the abduction issue and normalization is as yet unknown.

It is possible that Koizumi's decision to visit Pyongyang in 2002 was not only motivated by domestic politics, but also by a strategic calculation to ensure that Japan's voice on North Korean matters in the emerging regional diplomatic framework would be heard. By showing willingness (if neces-sary) to bilaterally pursue a comprehensive normalization of relations with North Korea at a time when the United States was contemplating a new regional security discussion framework (with a greater importance assigned to China), Koizumi likely assured Japan a seat in the emerging 6PT.

Furthermore, emerging strategic thinking in Japan's North Korea policy is evident in the way its crisis responses have been built into the long-term strategy of enhancing the US-Japan alliance. The North Korean crisis has served as a driver of Japan's "normalization" and pursuit of collective defense with the United States.[35]

NOTES

1. Yoshihide Soeya in detail documented Japan's efforts to nourish economic ties with the People's Republic of China through the 1950s and 1960s in *Japan's Economic Diplomacy with China, 1945–1978* (Oxford: Oxford University Press, 1999). For general analysis of Japan's diplomatic divergence from the United States, also see: Akitoshi Miyashita and Yoichiro Sato, eds., *Japanese Foreign Policy in Asia and the Pacific: Domestic Interests, American Pressure, and Regional Integration* (New York: Palgrave, 2001).

2. Linus Hagstrom and Marie Soderberg, eds., *North Korea Policy: Japan and the Great Powers* (London: Routledge, 2006).

3. Christopher W. Hughes, "The Political Economy of Japanese Sanctions towards North Korea: Domestic Coalitions and International Systemic Pressure," *Pacific Affairs* 79, no. 3 (Fall 2006): 455–81.

4. David Fouse, "Japan's Post-Cold War North Korea Policy: Hedging toward Autonomy?" in *Japan in a Dynamic Asia: Coping with the New Security Challenges*, eds. Yoichiro Sato and Satu Limaye (Lanham: Lexington Books, 2006), 135–55.

5. Yuki Tatsumi, ed., *North Korea: Challenge for the U.S.-Japan Alliance* (Washington, DC: Stimson Center, 2011). A more cynical view of this aspect of the North Korean crisis is seen in Christopher W. Hughes, "'Super-Sizing' the DPRK Threats: Japan's Evolving Military Posture and North Korea," *Asian Survey* 49, no. 2 (March/April 2009): 291–311.

6. Participation of the former Japanese naval officers in minesweeping opera-tions during the Korean War was a major exception this general statement. Hidetaka Suzuki, "Chosen kaiiki ni shutsugeki shita nihon tokubetsu soukaitai—sono hikari to kage [The Special Japanese Minesweeping Force

Deployed to Korean Waters—Its Glory and Shadow]," unpublished paper, n.d., accessed 1 February 2014, http://www.mod.go.jp/msdf/mf/history /img/004.pdf.

7. Tessa Morris-Suzuki, "The Forgotten Victims of the North Korean Crisis," *Pacific Forum Online*, Nautilus Institute, 07-022A, 13 March 2007, accessed 14 January 2014, http://web.archive.org/web/20070927012134/http://www .nautilus.org/fora/security/07022MorrisSuzuki.html.

8. Public Security Intelligence Agency (Japan), "Naigai jousei no kaiko to tenpou (heisei 20 nen 1 gatsu) [Reflections on and Prospects of the Internal and External Affairs (January 2008)]," accessed 27 January 2014, http:// www.moj.go.jp/psia/kouan_naigai_naigai20_naigai20-04.html.

9. Hidekazu Sakai, "Continuity and Discontinuity of Japanese Foreign Policy toward North Korea: Freezing the Korean Energy Development Organization (KEDO) in 1998," in Miyashita and Sato, *Japanese Foreign Policy*, 53–74.

10. Yoichiro Sato, "US North Korea Policy: The 'Japan factor'" in Hagstrom and Soderberg, *North Korea Policy*, 82.

11. Condoleezza Rice, *No Higher Honor: A Memoir of My Years in Washington* (New York: Broadway, 2011), 159.

12. Sato, "US North Korea policy," 82.

13. Yoichiro Sato, "Will the US-Japan Alliance Continue?" *New Zealand International Review* 24, no. 4 (July/August 1999): 10–12.

14. Rice, *No Higher Honor*, 524–25.

15. United Nations Security Council Resolution 1695(2006), 15 July 2006, S/RES/1695(2006), accessed 28 January 2014, http://www.un.org/en/ga /search/view_doc.asp?symbol=S/RES/1695(2006).

16. United Nations Security Council Resolution 1718(2006), 14 October 2006, S/RES/1718(2006), accessed 28 January 2014, http://www.un.org/en/ga /search/view_doc.asp?symbol=S/RES/1718(2006).

17. United Nations Security Council Resolution 1718(2006), 12 June 2009, S/RES/1874(2009), accessed 28 January 2014, http://www.un.org/en/ga /search/view_doc.asp?symbol=S/RES/1874(2009).

18. "Kokunai zenekon ga houchou keikaku—yoron ni hairyo shi toriyame [A plan to visit North Korea by general contractors—cancelled in consideration of the public opinion]," *47 News*, 21 October 2004, accessed 27 January 2014, http://www.47news.jp/CN/200410/CN2004102101001208.html.

19. Seongho Sheen, "Japan-South Korea Relations: Slowly Lifting the Burden of History?" in Sato and Limaye, eds., *Japan in a Dynamic Asia*, 117–34.

20. Victor Cha, *Alignment Despite Antagonism: The United States-Korea-Japan Security Triangle* (Stanford: Stanford University Press, 2000).

21. Robert M. Gates, *Duty: Memoirs of a Secretary at War* (New York: Alfred A. Knopf, 2014), 416.

22. "Beikan enshu ni kaiji kanbu haken, seifu kettei, obuzaba de [The government decides dispatching Maritime Self Defense Force senior officers to a US-Korea Exercise as observers]," *Nihon Keizai Shimbun*, 23 July 2010, accessed 31 August 2013, http://www.nikkei.com/article /DGXNASFS2301O_T20C10A7MM8000/.

23. Gates, *Duty*, 497.

24. Kentaro Ogura, "Iijima-shi, joretsu nii no Kim Yongnam shi to kaidan [Mr. Iijima has discussion with the second-ranked Mr. Kim Yongnam]," *Nihon Keizai Shimbun*, 17 May 2013, 4.

25. "Nicchou koukan, Vietnam de himitsu kyougi ka, nihon seifugawa wa hitei [High-ranking Japanese and North Korean officials may secretly talk in Vietnam—the Japanese government denies]," *Asahi Shimbun*, 28 January 2014, accessed 28 January 2014, http://www.asahi.com/articles /ASG1W7D4MG1WUHBI02M.html.

26. "Kita no wana ni hamatta Iijima-shi houchou, kaidan ni wa tainichi kousaku kikan kanbu mo douseki [The Iijima visit to North Korea was a trap. The meeting was also attended by key members of the anti-Japan special operatives agency]," *Sankei Shimbun*, 25 May 2013, accessed 25 January 2014, http://sankei.jp.msn.com/world/news/130525/kor13052518000008-n1.htm.

27. Steven R. Weisman, "Japan-Korea Pact Has Tokyo Astir," *New York Times*, 3 October 1990, accessed 14 January 2014. http://www.nytimes.com/1990/10 /03/world/japan-korea-pact-has-tokyo-astir.html.

28. Toshimitsu Shigemura, *Gaiko haiboku* [Diplomatic Defeat] (Tokyo: Kondansha, 2006), 94.

29. Yoshinori Murai, *Tettei kensho Nippon no ODA* [A Complete Examination of Japan's ODA] (Tokyo: Komonzu, 2006), 91–94.

30. Metropolitan Police Department (Tokyo), "Kitachousen ni yoru rachi yougi jian [Suspected cases of abductions by North Korea]," accessed 14 January 2014, http://www.keishicho.metro.tokyo.jp/jiken/rati/ratigian.htm.

31. Rice, *No Higher Honor*, 528, 648–49. Rice and her negotiator in the 6PT, Assistant Secretary of State Christopher Hill, saw Japan's abduction issue as a potential spoiler of the overall negotiation. Use of the Japanese abduction issue by the hardliners within the US government to prevent an agreement with North Korea was also a concern. See Sato, "US North Korea Policy," 86.

32. Rachi Mondai Sougou Taisaku Honbu Jimukyoku Sougou Chousei Shitsu [Secretariat of the Headquarter for Comprehensive Measures on the Abduction Issue, Overall Liaison Office], "Iizuka-ke to Kim Hyonhui-shi to no menkai (gaiyou) [Summary of the meeting between the Iizuka family and Ms. Kim Hyon-hui]," 12 March 2009, accessed 27 January 2014, http://www.rachi.go.jp/jp/archives/2009/0311menkai.pdf.

33. "Hasuike Toru-shi 'rachi mondai wa seisai dewa kaiketsu shinai' to Abe shushou ni chokugen [Toru Hasuike told Prime Minister Abe 'the abduction issue would not be solved through sanctions'], *Asahi.dot*, 14 February 2013 accessed 27 January 2014, http://dot.asahi.com/news/domestic/2013021300011 .html; Sebastian Maslow, "An End to the 'Lost Decade' in Japan-North Korea Relations?" *Diplomat*, 7 May 2014, accessed 16 September 2014, http://thediplomat.com/2014/05/an-end-to-the-lost-decade-in-japan -north-korea-relations/.

34. Maslow, "An End to the 'Lost Decade.'"

35. Japan first worked on limited bilateral military cooperation outside Japan's territorial defense through sunset legislation and then worked on amending the permanent laws governing Japan's territorial defense and the role of the Self Defense Forces in cooperation with the US forces. For progress of collective defense between Japan and the United States and the associated legal discussions during the last two decades, see Yoichiro Sato, "Three Norms of Collective Defense and Japan's Overseas Troop Dispatches," in *Norms, Interests, and Power in Japanese Foreign Policy*, eds. Yoichiro Sato and Keiko Hirata (New York: Palgrave Macmillan, 2008), 93–108; Clint Richards, "Japan: De Facto Approval of Collective Self-Defense," *Diplomat*, 16 July 2014, accessed 16 September 2014, http://thediplomat.com/2014/07 /japan-de-facto-approval-of-collective-self-defense/.

CHAPTER 9

North Korea's Nuclear Weapons and the United States

More Difficult, More Complicated, and More Dangerous

Nicholas HAMISEVICZ

The Democratic People's Republic of Korea (DPRK, or North Korea) has been called the impossible state and the land of lousy options. About to complete his third full year as leader of North Korea, Kim Jong Un continues to try to push the country into pursuing advances in both military and economic spheres, what has been called the Byungjin ("in tandem") line. Improvements in North Korea's missile and nuclear weapons capabilities along with some changes in economic emphasis create, from a perspective of the United States government, a situation where those lousy options are rapidly becoming even worse. Furthermore, avenues for the United States to improve relations with North Korea, both bilaterally and with multilateral partners in the region, become narrower, less certain of the destination, and loaded with roadblocks and potential dead ends with serious political and security implications for the United States, the Asia-Pacific region, and the world. Two issues have made things more difficult for the United States: North Korea's nuclear weapons and missile technology are improving, and

North Korea's rejection of condition offers for engagement by the United States and South Korea have given their respective leaders less flexibility to reach out to North Korea in the future. These dynamics significantly impact how the United States can interact, approach, and deal with North Korea to eliminate its nuclear weapons and missile programs.

Nuclear weapons and missiles could be the most dangerous of the numerous ways North Korea can threaten the United States, its allies, and the rest of the global community. North Korea has both plutonium and uranium programs for developing nuclear weapons. After its third nuclear weapons test in 2013, North Korea claimed it had a "miniaturized and lighter nuclear device," suggesting it had the capability of miniaturizing the nuclear weapon for delivery on a missile.[1] To complicate the nature of North Korea's nuclear weapons program even more, the government revised its constitution to say North Korea is "a nuclear-armed state and an indomitable military power."[2] Now the United States will have to negotiate away something that is enshrined in the North Korean constitution.

North Korea is also improving its missile capabilities, aiming to deploy a reliable means of striking the United States with a nuclear weapon. While North Korea has short- and medium-range missiles that can target US bases in South Korea and Japan, until recently North Korea lacked the capability to hit Guam and the continental United States. Unfortunately, this may no longer be the case. In 2011, then US Secretary of Defense Robert Gates said North Korea would be able to hit the continental United States within five years with an intercontinental ballistic missile. One year later, North Korea tested a missile that launched a satellite into space. Recovery of the debris from that launch had South Korea's defense officials believing the missile could travel "more than 10,000 km."[3]

North Korea also has road-mobile launchers that can fire a class of intercontinental ballistic missile that, according to some analysts, "probably does have the range to reach the United States."[4] North Korea is getting close, if it hasn't done so already, to developing a durable missile cone that could transport a miniaturized nuclear warhead.[5] There is still some skepticism that North Korea's ground and road-mobile missiles have attained this capability. Despite uncertainty about when the DPRK will have the full range of weaponized missile technology, North Korea's missile threat to the US is no longer theoretical but a "practical consideration" in the words of General Charles Jacoby, chief of the North American Aerospace Defense Command.[6]

The United States and South Korea have tried in some ways to improve relations with North Korea. Both in campaigning to become president and shortly after his re-election for a second term, Barack Obama said the United States would reach out its hand if only North Korea would unclench its fist. North Korea's responses were a nuclear test in May 2009 and the December 2012 missile and satellite launch.[7] The breakdown of the 29 February 2012 deal and North Korea's imprisonment of American citizens also contributed to the Obama administration's unwillingness to upgrade relations without North Korea addressing US concerns on nuclear and missile issues.

Park Geun-hye pushed her *trustpolitik* policy and offered ideas for better inter-Korea relations during her campaign for the presidency of South Korea. Yet almost two weeks before Park was sworn in as president, North Korea treated the incoming administration to a nuclear test, forcing her to begin her presidency responding to a North Korean provocation rather than developing an opportunity for inter-Korea dialogue. After tough negotiations North and South Korea carried out a reunion of separated family members. North Korea, however, rebuffed the Park administration's desire for regularized family visits in the future. This rejection by North Korea further limited Park Geun-hye's flexibility for finding other opportunities to expand inter-Korea connections.

NATIONAL INTERESTS AT STAKE FOR THE UNITED STATES

The North Korea nuclear weapons issue involves many short-term security problems for the United States. North Korea has used the testing of nuclear weapons and the threat of using nuclear weapons as provocations to induce engagement, to extract economic aid or support, to demand diplomatic recognition, and to undermine US alliances. All of the US military bases in Japan and South Korea, along with many American businesses and people that live, work, and travel to these countries, are within range of

North Korea's missiles. In addition to the need to protect these assets, the United States must maintain its credibility as a protector of its allies Japan and South Korea.

Another immediate US objective is nonproliferation. The US government wants to reduce the appeal of the North Korea example to other countries contemplating building their own nuclear weapons. North Korea's deployment of nuclear weapons in defiance of US warnings undercuts current US negotiations with Iran, possibly providing additional confidence to Teheran and other governments not to succumb to US pressure.

It is not just its example that promotes proliferation; North Korea is actually collaborating with other countries in building nuclear weapons and long-range missiles. The US Department of Defense said one of its "gravest concerns" about North Korea is "its demonstrated willingness to proliferate nuclear technology."[8] North Korea and Iran have worked together on their nuclear and missile programs, have exchanged nuclear scientists, and have completed deals to transfer weapons. The two countries also signed a science and technology agreement similar to a deal North Korea and Syria made in 2002 that led to the Syrians nearly producing a nuclear reactor undetected.[9] The George W. Bush administration was divided over how to deal with the plutonium reactor North Korea helped Syria build. Eventually, in September 2007, Israel bombed and destroyed the reactor.[10] With Syria engulfed in an inconclusive civil war, North Korea's past connections with supplying weapons to Syria brings concern that the Syrian government could use North Korea–supplied weapons in another massacre.[11]

North Korea has sought out nuclear technology cooperation with other countries outside of the Middle East as well. Part of North Korea's nuclear and missile success was because of the interaction it had with Pakistan and the A. Q. Khan network. North Korea also had a relationship with Burma (Myanmar). When the United States expanded relations with Burma under the Obama administration, Washington asked Burma to reduce its military ties with North Korea and in particular to desist from any involvement in North Korea missile or nuclear technology trafficking. There is some concern that Burma might have kept a few channels open to these dangerous programs. The US Treasury Department's blacklisting of Lieutenant-General Thein Htay for conducting illicit military arms trade with North Korea and the seizure of aluminum alloy rods that could be used for making nuclear centrifuges suggest there are still some possibly dangerous connections between North Korea and Burma.[12]

The US government fears North Korea could reach beyond state-to-state interaction to provide weapons expertise to non-state actors and terrorist organizations. Recently a US District Court judge ruled that North Korea "had worked in concert with Iran and Syria to provide rocket and missile components to Hezbollah" in the Middle East.[13]

In addition to the security and political concerns, a breakout of violence on the Korean Peninsula would be extremely damaging for the United States' and South Korea's economies as well as the regional and world economies. When tensions were high on the Korean Peninsula last year after North Korea began closing operations at the Kaesong Industrial Complex, General Motors (GM) CEO Dan Akerson said that his company was making contingency plans to get GM workers out of Korea if North Korean provocations escalated.[14] Even absent a major military conflict, a period of persistent high tensions could force foreign businesses to rethink their operations in South Korea.

For the United States government, promoting respect for human rights globally is a major national interest and component of US foreign policy. North Korea's abysmal human rights record also stands in the way of better relations with the United States and the international community. North Korea's frequent incarceration of American citizens on questionable grounds further antagonizes Washington. These human rights issues complicate the US government's ability to find ways to address North Korea's nuclear weapons program. The recent United Nations Commission of Inquiry Report on Human Rights in the Democratic People's Republic of Korea, along with recent books such as *Nothing to Envy* and *Escape from Camp 14* that recall the difficult circumstances defectors faced inside North Korea, has brought unprecedented attention to the scale of the country's human rights problem. Thus, US human rights policy toward North Korea and its denuclearization efforts could be more closely linked. Improvement on human rights and the return of US citizens would remove one of the obstacles preventing an improvement in the US-DPRK relationship.

In the long term, the United States wants to see a reduction of nuclear weapons around the world. The Obama administration says it aspires to a nuclear weapons–free world. His promotion of nuclear nonproliferation was one of the reasons President Obama was awarded the Nobel Peace Prize in 2009. This goal is also closely intertwined with the long-term US interest in maintaining an international order that regulates, monitors, and enforces universal norms. There is a global nonproliferation regime made up of organizations, laws, and resolutions to help prevent nuclear and missile proliferation and escalation. The Non-Proliferation Treaty on Nuclear Weapons (NPT) attempted to prevent the spread of nuclear weapons and technology. North Korea's withdrawal from the NPT set a bad precedent and hurt international cooperation on nonproliferation.

North Korea's possession of nuclear weapons is an obstacle to Korean reunification. If countries in the region have reservations about a unified Korea, these reservations are greater if that unified Korea was sure to have nuclear weapons. Moreover, if the United States and countries in the region were able to get North Korea to give up its nuclear weapons, this would eliminate the potential danger of a race to seize and control those nuclear weapons and materials by special forces from China, South Korea, and the United States during a collapse of North Korea scenario. A long-term interest of the United States is to keep the unification process as peaceful as possible. A peaceful process is much less likely with North Korea in possession of nuclear weapons.

DEBATES AND IDEAS

Debates continue in the United States on how to best address the growing difficulty of dealing with North Korea's threats to US interests in the region. The engagement versus deterrence debate still dominates the discussions about handling North Korea. While proponents of either side acknowledge both aspects are needed with North Korea, the arguments focus on which of these is most effective in getting North Korea to change its behavior. The growing threat from North Korea only strengthens the resolve of advocates on each side. For those in favor of more engagement, multiple points of interaction should be used for engagement because the American with the most access in North Korea shouldn't be Dennis Rodman, a former NBA basketball player.

For those who favor more deterrence and pressure, only stronger military coordination and sanctions against North Korea will make the leadership take new positions more favorable for normal relations with the international community. The feeling that North Korea has pursued nuclear weapons and missiles even during times of engagement suggests to this camp that concessions without reciprocity will not elicit the desired response from North Korea.

However, North Korea's successes in its nuclear and missile programs have caused a new debate to start forming on the advantages and disadvantages of waiting out North Korea. Despite a willingness by the United States and South Korea to wait for a better opportunity to engage, advances in North Korea's missile and nuclear weapons programs put pressure on the "strategic patience" and *trustpolitik* plans offered by Presidents Obama and Park. Each technological success of North Korea further complicates the situation, making the direct threat to the United States even more imminent. This timing discussion then connects back with the engagement versus pressure debate: because the threat to the United States has increased, Washington can't afford to wait and must immediately either engage North Korea or increase the pressure on North Korea to give up its weapons.

The debate on how to handle North Korea also includes a debate on US-China relations. China's ties to North Korea stem from the experience of fighting together in the Korean War, a growing economic relationship, and party and government interactions. These increasing ties have forced countries into acceding that any movement with North Korea, especially on nuclear weapons, will require help from China. Thus, as the US and China try to navigate a future where the two powers interact more across political and economic spheres, North Korea continues to be an area where the two sides have different interests. This causes contentious discussions on how each side should be doing more to convince North Korea it needs to cease provocations and eventually give up its nuclear weapons.

Whatever the debates may be regarding North Korea, there will likely be less disagreement on the most appealing solution to the United States. A deal that provides a clear, quick path toward denuclearization and elimination of the long-range missile threat would likely be close to an ideal solution for the United States. This agreement would also have to include extremely good monitoring access of the dismantlement of both the missile and nuclear weapons programs. Ideally, North Korea's leadership would accept language similar to what was in the 29 February 2012 "Leap Day" agreement, wherein the United States government "reaffirms that it does not have any hostile intent toward the DPRK," as a security guarantee.[15] North Korea would likely require some financial incentives to make a deal; the United States would probably insist this aid be in a form that could be monitored. The United States could probably make an agreement where some sanctions it has placed on North Korea are removed; however, the United States would benefit greatly by having these sanction reductions occur later in the process after the dismantling of the weapons programs. This solution would be even more appealing if the US government felt it would eventually help lead to peaceful unification under the principles of freedom, democracy, and a free market economy. These are values President Obama and South Korea Presidents Park Geun-hye and Lee Myung Bak identified as important for unification.[16]

While an optimal solution would likely have those components, finding the minimum aspects Washington would require to accept an agreement with North Korea would be difficult. Part of this complexity is that the North Korea threat against the United States has dramatically increased. Thus, a minimum ask from the United States a decade ago is unlikely to fulfill the minimum requirement of today.

Finally, in light of North Korea's record of noncompliance with treaties and agreements, combined with its attempts to evade monitoring of its nuclear and missile programs, Washington would likely need some ability to verify the closure of North Korea's weapons development programs.

With all sides appearing to be at an impasse, Washington, Pyongyang, and Seoul have been investigating compromise positions that might lead to a diplomatic solution. Envoys for nations involved in the Six-Party Talks have been traveling across the region trying to find an answer. Senior officials in the Obama administration still state they are waiting for North Korea to demonstrate a commitment to implementing the September 2005 statement and to create a path toward denuclearization.[17]

The timing of respective moves by Pyongyang and Washington could allow for flexibility on the US side. While the phrase "complete, verifiable, and irreversible dismantlement" of North Korea's nuclear weapons programs was associated with the Bush administration, these are still the general aspects of a deal the US government seeks. Because of the difficulty in actually getting movement on any of those features, one could envision an understanding along the lines of a freeze on North Korea building nuclear weapons and missiles. This idea was the basis of the 29 February 2012 agreement. The statement released by the United States had North Korea agreeing to "implement a moratorium on long-range missile launches, nuclear tests and nuclear activities at Yongbyon, including uranium enrichment activities" while the United States would provide North Korea with 240,000 metric tons of nutritional assistance.[18] However, this deal was never implemented because one month later, North Korea announced it would attempt to put a satellite into space. Washington and much of the international community argued the launch was actually a missile test in violation of UN prohibitions on the DPRK. The US declared the Leap Day agreement nullified; less than two months later, the DPRK satellite launch ended in failure as well.

Many policy analysts argue a moratorium is not only possible, but is also the best deal the outside world is likely to get. Siegfried Hecker, former Director of Los Alamos National Laboratory and a Stanford University professor, has put forth an idea of the "three noes: no export, no more bombs, and no better bombs."[19] In November 2010, Dr. Hecker was invited to North Korea and was surprised to be shown a "modern uranium centrifuge facility at Yongbyon" with two thousand centrifuges that were "said to be producing low enriched uranium (LEU) destined for fuel for the new reactor."[20] After the revelation of this facility to Dr. Hecker, calculations started to change, as it was clear that North Korea had a uranium-enrichment program that could begin producing highly enriched uranium (HEU) necessary for a nuclear weapon, and that North Korea probably had another hidden uranium-enrichment facility.

Ambassador Stephen Bosworth, former US Ambassador to South Korea and former Special Representative for North Korea Policy, made an argument similar to Hecker's. Bosworth asserted that verifying North Korea's complete dismantlement of its nuclear facilities and its missile capabilities would be an impossible task. Thus, he recommended a "standstill agreement" where North Korea would cease conducting nuclear tests and missile launches, which would in turn be easier for the United States and the international community to monitor.[21]

Some suggest an even longer path of engagement before North Korea would give up its nuclear weapons. Frank Jannuzi, President and CEO of the Maureen and Mike Mansfield Foundation, advocated for a longer "Helsinki-style engagement strategy" entailing numerous connections for dialogue and cooperation.[22] Jannuzi hoped this process would bring about confidence-building measures along with opportunities for collaboration on other issues.[23] He argued that a foundation of trust and understanding must precede efforts toward the denuclearization of North Korea.

In the absence of a moratorium on North Korea's nuclear weapons and missile launches, Pyongyang continues to improve its capabilities. As the DPRK's weapons become more capable, it is more difficult for the US government to agree to a freeze that would allow North Korea to keep weapons in the short term in hopes that the longer process would lead to eventual dismantlement. The Leap Day agreement was an attempt at a moratorium-like deal to break the impasse; the deal's collapse reduced the political capital within the Obama administration to attempt new ways to engage North Korea. These factors, along with North Korean provocations toward the United States and South Korea and Pyongyang's refusal to release captive US citizens, reduce the space for finding a nuanced way to reach the goal of a denuclearized North Korea.

IS THERE ANY POSSIBLE PATH TO DENUCLEARIZATION?

Nuance, flexibility, and cooperation will be needed to convince North Korea to abandon its nuclear and missile programs. All five countries in the region along with the international community must begin to work harder to coordinate policy and pressure North Korea into maintaining consistent, positive interaction with its neighboring countries rather than the cycle it usually employs: provocation followed by a charm offensive.

A first step in that coordination should be encouraging North Korea to engage in consistent and positive engagement with South Korea. Better inter-Korea relations will be important for sustaining connections with North Korea, determining its willingness to interact with the international community, and reducing tensions on the Korean peninsula. Family reunions, expansion of the Kaesong Industrial Complex, cooperation over joint fishing areas, and expanding tourism areas are all inter-Korea projects that have not fully materialized; these efforts need more support in order to create a better environment for cooperation. With a reduction in tensions between the two Koreas, all sides and relevant parties gain more flexibility to work on the difficult issues of missiles and nuclear weapons.

In order to make progress on those difficult issues, better coordination and commitment is needed among the United States, China, Russia, South Korea, and Japan to develop both incentives and punishments for North Korea's actions. The countries already have their envoys trying to figure out a framework for moving forward with North Korea. The five countries should begin meeting together as a group in Beijing, where the Six-Party Talks are officially held. If the five countries find it too provocative toward North Korea to all meet together at one time, envoys from the United States and China respectively should take it upon themselves to practice shuttle diplomacy. The US envoy could meet with his South Korean and Japanese counterparts in Seoul or Tokyo in the morning, and then fly to Beijing and meet with his Chinese and Russian counterparts in the afternoon. The following meeting, the Chinese envoy could reciprocate. The goal would be to illustrate to North Korea that the region sees North Korea's nuclear weapons as a threat to stability. While little consensus may be achieved, North Korea needs to see that the other countries will move ahead even if North Korea doesn't want to rejoin the talks.

Despite the small possibility of consensus, the five countries should try to develop an understanding about responses to a nuclear test and a multistage missile test, such as a general agreement on taking the issue immediately to the United Nations Security Council and reducing aid to and trade with North Korea. Adding to the sanctions on North Korea would increase the cost to Pyongyang of refusing to denuclearize.[24] Even a multinational agreement on broad terms would be helpful in reducing the avenues North Korea uses to exploit rifts and divide the other countries' efforts to solve the nuclear weapons crisis. The coordination need not be limited to coercive pressure. The five countries should also develop an understanding of the various aid packages each would be willing to provide to North Korea should Pyongyang decide to change course.

However, this is a very unlikely scenario. The level of coordination that would yield even a basic multilateral agreement of shared principles would be unprecedented. More likely, each country's interests and goals would take precedence, leading to five different approaches along with some loose interconnections between the efforts of the United States, South Korea, and Japan. North Korea will try to play all sides off each other, buying time to continue developing its nuclear and missile programs while hoping trade from China and international aid provides just enough economic support to sustain the DPRK economy and regime. Unfortunately, this means the difficulties in reaching a negotiated solution to the crisis will only worsen.

North Korea's nuclear weapons and missile programs have improved. These successes, along with the lack of receptivity to conditional engagement efforts by the United States and South Korea, have made trying to solve the North Korea nuclear problem more difficult for the United States. This difficulty increases with the passage of time as North Korea continues its weapons development programs while Washington waits for an encouraging DPRK response. For the United States, the path toward North Korea's denuclearization will likely remain narrow, difficult, and dangerous.

NOTES

1. "North Korea Confirms 'Successful' Nuclear Test: KCNA," Reuters, 12 February 12, 2013, accessed 26 July 2014, http://www.reuters.com /article/2013/02/12/us-korea-north-kcna-idUSBRE91B07I20130212.

2. "N.K. Calls Itself 'Nuclear-armed State' in Revised Constitution," Yonhap News, 30 May 2012, accessed 26 July 2014, http://www.koreaherald.com /view.php?ud=20120530001382&cpv=0. The section in the preamble of the North Korean constitution that mentions North Korea as a "nuclear-armed state" is available in Korean at http://www.naenara.com.kp/ko/great /constitution.php?1 (accessed 26 July 2014).

3. "S. Korea Says Debris Reveals North's ICBM Technology," *Voice of America*, 23 December 2012, accessed 26 July 2014, http://www.voanews.com/content /north-korea-missile/1570703.html.

4. Park Hyun, "US to Boost Missile Defense in Response to North Korean Threats," *Hankyoreh*, 18 March 2013, accessed 26 July 2014, http://english .hani.co.kr/arti/ENGISSUE/102/578507.html; and Office of the Secretary of Defense, "Military and Security Developments Involving the Democratic People's Republic of Korea 2013," accessed 26 July 2014, http://www .defense.gov/pubs/North_Korea_Military_Power_Report_2013-2014.pdf. North Korea calls the missiles that would be used on these mobile launchers Hwasong-13 missiles, while the US military and others have designated them as KN-08 missiles.

5. Jeong Yong-soo and Kang Jin-kyu, "US, Korea See Larger Nuclear Threat," *Joongang Ilbo*, 29 August 2013, accessed 26 July 2014, http:// koreajoongangdaily.joins.com/news/article/article.aspx?aid=2976819; and Eli Lake, "US Recovery of North Korean Satellite Exposed Nuclear Progress," *Telegraph*, 15 April 2013, accessed 26 July 2014, http://www .telegraph.co.uk/journalists/the-daily-beast/9995514/US-recovery-of -North-Korean-satellite-exposed-nuclear-progress.html.

6. General Charles H. Jacoby, Jr., Statement before the Committee on Armed Services, US Senate, 13 March 2014, accessed 26 July 2014, http://www .armed-services.senate.gov/imo/media/doc/Jacoby_03-13-14.pdf.

7. Nicholas Hamisevicz, "No Illusions for North Korea," *National Bureau of Asian Research Commentary*, 12 February 2013, accessed 26 July 2014, http:// www.nbr.org/research/activity.aspx?id=308.

8. Office of the Secretary of Defense "Military and Security Developments."

9. Ali Akbar Dareini, "Iran, North Korea Sign Technology Agreement," Associated Press, 2 September 2012, accessed 26 July 2014, http://news .yahoo.com/iran-north-korea-sign-technology-agreement-104143016.html; Claudia Rosett, "Iran's Sequel to North Korea's Nuclear Playbook," *Forbes*, 7 October 2013, accessed 26 July 2014, at http://www.forbes.com/sites /claudiarosett/2013/10/07/irans-sequel-to-north-koreas-nuclear-playbook/.

10. David E. Sanger and Mark Mazzetti, "Israel Struck Syrian Nuclear Project, Analysts Say," *New York Times*, 14 October 2007, accessed 26 July 2014, http://www.nytimes.com/2007/10/14/washington/14weapons.html ?pagewanted=all&_r=0; Elliott Abrams, "Bombing the Syrian Reactor: The Untold Story," *Commentary Magazine*, 1 February 2013, accessed 26 July 2014, http://www.commentarymagazine.com/article/bombing-the-syrian -reactor-the-untold-story/; and Office of the Secretary of Defense, "Military and Security Developments."

11. Alexandre Mansourov, "North Korea: Entering Syria's Civil War," *38 North*, 25 November 2013, accessed 26 July 2014, http://38north.org/2013/11 /amansourov112513/.

12. US Department of the Treasury, "Treasury Designates Burmese L.T. General Thein Htay, Chief of Directorate of Defense Industries," 2 July 2013, accessed 2 September 2014, http://www.treasury.gov/press-center/press -releases/Pages/jl1998.aspx; and "'Centrifuge Rods' from North Korea Seized from Ship in Tokyo," *AFP-JIJI*, 19 March 2013, accessed 2 September 2014, http://www.japantimes.co.jp/news/2013/03/19/national/centrifuge-rods -from-north-korea-seized-from-ship-in-tokyo/#.VAXHHWMfLcT.

13. Office of the Secretary of Defense, "Military and Security Developments."

14. Zach Bowman, "GM's Akerson Mulling South Korea Exit Options Due to North Korean Tensions," 4 April 2013, http://www.autoblog.com/2013/04 /04/gms-akerson-mulling-south-korea-exit-options-due-to-north-korea/.

15. US Department of State, "US-DPRK Bilateral Discussions," 29 February 2012, accessed 26 July 2014, http://www.state.gov/r/pa/prs/ps/2012/02 /184869.htm.

16. The Obama administration has been clear in espousing these principles it would like to see in a unified Korea. See "Joint Vision for the Alliance of the United States of America and the Republic of Korea," The White House, 16 June 2009, accessed 26 July 2014, at http://www.whitehouse.gov/the_press _office/Joint-vision-for-the-alliance-of-the-United-States-of-America-and- the-Republic-o f-Korea/ and "Joint Declaration in the Commemoration of the 60th Anniversary of the Alliance between the Republic of Korea and the United States of America," The White House, 7 May 2013, accessed 26 July 2014, at http://www.whitehouse.gov/the-press-office/2013/05/07/joint -declaration-commemoration-60th-anniversary -alliance-between-republ.

17. "Remarks at the Westin Chaoyang Hotel," US Department of State, 28 January 2014, accessed 26 July 2014, at http://www.state.gov/p/eap/rls/rm /2014/01/220703.htm.

18. "US-DPRK Bilateral Discussions," US Department of State, 29 February 2012, accessed 26 July 2014, at http://www.state.gov/r/pa/prs/ps/2012/02 /184869.htm.

19. Siegfried Hecker, "Extraordinary Visits," *The Nonproliferation Review*, June 2011, Vol. 18:2, 445–55, accessed 26 July 2014, at http://dx.doi.org/10.1080 /10736700.2011.583122.

20. Siegfried Hecker, "Extraordinary Visits," *The Nonproliferation Review*, June 2011, Vol. 18:2, 445–55, accessed 26 July 2014, at http://dx.doi.org/10.1080 /10736700.2011.583122, and Siegfried S. Hecker, "North Korea's Yongbyon

Nuclear Complex: A Report by Siegfried S. Hecker," Center for International Security and Cooperation, Stanford University, 20 November 2010, accessed 26 July 2014, at cisac.stanford.edu/publications/north_koreas_yongbyon _nuclear_complex_a_report_by_siegfried_s_hecker.

21. Evan Ramstad, "Bosworth: Get Real on CVID," *Wall Street Journal*, 18 September 2012, accessed 26 July 2014, at http://blogs.wsj.com /korearealtime/2012/09/18/bosworth-get-real-on-the-v-in-cvid/.

22. Frank Januzzi, "Putting People Before Plutonium," *38 North*, 11 December 2013, accessed 26 July 2014, at http://38north.org/2013/12/fjannuzi121113/.

23. Frank Januzzi, "Putting People Before Plutonium."

24. For a list of sanctions the United States could possibly still employ, see Bruce Klingner, "Time to Get North Korean Sanctions Right," Heritage Foundation, Backgrounder #2850, 4 November 2013, accessed 26 July 2014, at http://www.heritage.org/research/reports/2013/11/time-to-get-north -korean-sanctions-right.

CHAPTER 10

Unwitting Bedfellows

Taiwan and the North Korea Problem

Ching-Chang CHEN

It may look strange to include a chapter on Taiwan in a monograph that examines regional responses to the security challenges and humanitarian issues posed by the Democratic People's Republic of Korea (DPRK).[1] After all, Taiwan has not been involved in the Six-Party Talks and has never been named by Pyongyang as a potential target of its missile strikes. Nor is it conceivable that the island would be flooded with North Korean "boat people" in any worst-case scenario. Even though Taiwan appears to be a remote audience as far as the security situation on the Korean Peninsula is concerned, it is by no means irrelevant if regional stakeholders are to manage the North Korea issue effectively. The apparent differences in their national image (a prosperous fledging democracy vis-à-vis an impoverished Stalinist state) notwithstanding, they have something in common: both have acquired a rare, pariah-like status in post–Cold War East Asia. To be sure, Taiwan's exclusion from the international community has to do with its complicated relationship with the Chinese mainland, whereas the DPRK's isolation is to a large extent self-imposed. The two cases are, however, closely interrelated, for their isolation points to the unsettled (and increasingly tense) security competition between the United States and the People's Republic of China (PRC). Hostility accumulated during the Korean War and the lost chance to finish off the exiled Republic of China (ROC) forces in Taiwan had

prohibited the normalization of Beijing's diplomatic ties with Washington
for almost three decades. Historically, indeed, only when both the North
Korea issue and the Taiwan issue are absorbed into the background or given
less significance by the United States and the PRC can their security relations in East Asia be cordial.

Given the deeply intertwined trajectory of these two regional hotspots
since the onset of the Cold War in Asia, this chapter argues that the handling of these two issues cannot be entirely separated from each other. The
remainder of this chapter consists of four sections. The first and second
sections seek to locate the relationship between Taiwan and North Korea
in its historical and contemporary contexts. On that basis, the third section
examines Taipei's typically low-key policy toward Pyongyang, analyzing the
extent to which Taiwan represents a loophole in international sanctions
against North Korea. In the concluding section, the feasibility as to how
the United States and the PRC might "trade" their respective interests in
Taiwan and North Korea will be evaluated.

AN UNEXPECTED HISTORICAL CONNECTION

Kenneth Waltz's observation that "the fates of all the states . . . in a system
are affected much more by the acts and the interactions of the major ones
than of the minor ones"[2] explains why scholars of international relations
tend to pay considerable attention to the great powers' strategic behavior.
The fate of Chiang Kai-shek's ROC, however, was affected (and spared) as
much by North Korean troops' move to cross the 38th parallel as by a US
"reverse course" to incorporate Taiwan into its post-war "hub-and-spoke"
system. The Harry Truman administration issued its China White Paper in
August 1949, concluding that the demoralized Kuomintang (KMT, Chinese
Nationalist Party) had already lost the civil war and was too incompetent
to be saved by more US economic and military aid. Hoping to improve
its relationship with the newly established PRC and split it away from
the Soviet Union, the US government further announced in January 1950
that it would no longer provide military aid or advice to the remnants of
ROC forces on Taiwan. To make matters worse for the KMT, US military

assistance was not restored even after the PRC forged an alliance with the Soviet Union in February 1950, following Mao Zedong's earlier declaration that China would "lean to one side" toward Moscow. It was widely expected that the nascent yet victorious People's Liberation Army (PLA) would soon overcome the Taiwan Strait's "stopping power of water"[3] and conquer the island later that same year; the prospect was so bleak that Washington ordered nonessential US personnel in Taiwan to be evacuated on May 26.[4]

The outbreak of the Korean War on 25 June 1950 brought about a drastic reversal of US policy toward Taiwan, from virtually acquiescing to a Chinese Communist Party (CCP) total victory over the KMT to guaranteeing the island's security under US military protection. For Washington, the Sino-Soviet communist bloc had passed beyond the use of subversion in favor of war; under these circumstances, the communist occupation of Taiwan would represent a direct threat to the security of the Pacific area and to the United States.[5] When the Truman administration announced two days later that the United States would intervene to rescue the Republic of Korea (ROK), the Seventh Fleet was also ordered to patrol the Taiwan Strait, rendering the imminent PLA assault on Taiwan impossible. That Washington convinced the United Nations (UN) Security Council to condemn North Korea as an aggressor and to launch UN-authorized military intervention in defense of South Korea has been a well-known episode of the history of the Korean War.

The absence of Soviet opposition at the time, however, has to do with the sparring between the ROC and the Soviet bloc states in the UN. Losing the civil war, the Chinese Nationalists complained to the General Assembly that the Soviets were obstructing their efforts in reestablishing national authority in Manchuria after Japan's surrender by aiding the CCP with captured Japanese armaments.[6] The Soviet representative to the Security Council, Jacob A. Malik, countered in January 1950 by demanding his ROC counterpart yield the China seat to a PRC delegate. Malik walked out in protest after the council rejected his demand, claiming Moscow would boycott the council until Taipei was expelled. That absence proved crucial for the subsequent development of the Korean War.

But Truman's support for the KMT was limited. Washington held that Chiang's remaining troops should cease attacks against the mainland (so that ROC forces could concentrate on the defense of Taiwan) and that the future status of Taiwan was not yet settled (since a "two Chinas" policy could better justify Washington's intervention in denying the island to the PRC). The US position ran against the KMT regime's core claim that it remained the sole legitimate government of the whole China of which Taiwan is a part; without this claim, the ROC would look like a foreign government in exile, losing political legitimacy in the eyes of both the local Taiwanese and mainland Chinese refugees. Hence Taipei repeatedly requested US support for a large-scale military campaign to regain control of China, but Washington refused in each case.[7] The disagreement over the feasibility of the KMT's plan to reconquer China was played out in the idea of ROC troops fighting in Korea, which contributed to the dismissal of Douglas McArthur as UN forces commander in chief. Soon after hostilities began, Taipei offered to send 33,000 soldiers to fight under the UN banner. McArthur saw the ROC as a useful anti-communist asset and supported Taipei's proposal, whereas the Truman administration wanted to minimize PRC antagonism and declined Chiang's offer. Following the PLA's entry into the war (under the disguise of "volunteers"), McArthur again indicated his support for a US-ROC military alliance and allowing ROC forces to attack the mainland, an attempt to divert the PLA's attention away from Korea and reduce pressure on UN troops. Fearing the expansion of the war into mainland China would draw in Beijing's new alliance partner the Soviet Union, Truman relieved the general of his UN command in April 1951.

Despite these differing positions, Washington and Taipei took steps to strengthen their security cooperation after the outbreak of the Korean War. By the end of 1951, a US embassy was established in Taipei, the US Congress had approved a bill providing $300 million in aid to Taiwan, and a general was appointed to head the US military assistance group. Unlike his predecessor, moreover, Dwight Eisenhower welcomed Chiang as an ally and went so far as to declare in his first State of the Union address that Washington would no longer restrain ROC attacks against PRC forces.[8] As Korean War peace talks evolved, in May 1953 Chiang proposed to the Eisenhower administration a massive attack on the Chinese mainland to exploit Beijing's vulnerability if the talks failed. He also agreed to place ROC troops under the command of a US general if the United States participated. Although the armistice in July halted US consideration of this proposal, the KMT scored a political victory over the CCP at the end of the conflict. After Beijing dropped its insistence that Chinese and North Korean prisoners of war be repatriated to their home countries, Taipei delivered welcome letters and gifts to encourage defection; more than fourteen thousand out of a total of twenty thousand Chinese war prisoners, many of them former KMT soldiers, chose to go to Taiwan.[9] Strategically, Taipei also benefited from the timing of the Korean War and the subsequent "neutralization" of the Taiwan Strait, which provided the newly defeated ROC forces with a crucial window of opportunity to breathe and fortify offshore islands outside the coast of PRC-held Fujian Province. In December 1954, the United States and the ROC concluded a mutual defense treaty; the former formally included Taiwan in its "hub-and-spoke" alliance system without committing itself to the latter's proclaimed mission to "recover" the mainland. Lacking power-projection and amphibious landing capabilities in the 1950s, Beijing similarly came to realize that the post–Korean War international environment was no longer conducive to the "liberation" of Taiwan by force.[10] Not unlike the two Koreas, the rival regimes on the two sides of the Taiwan Strait in the early Cold War period felt bitter about their respective inability to revise the "two-China" status quo to their favor.

TAIWAN'S RELATIONS WITH NORTH KOREA

Because the ROC had supported the restoration of an independent Korea free from Japan's colonial rule, Chiang's government swiftly recognized the ROK after its establishment in August 1948. Even though ROC troops were excluded from combat in Korea, Taiwan supplied materials to the South. On the other hand, South Korea set up its embassy in Taipei right after the KMT's retreat to Taiwan, the only country that had diplomatic relations with the ROC to do so. Many South Korean political and military leaders, including presidents Syngman Rhee and Park Chung Hee, visited Chiang in Taiwan. Seeing South Koreans as brother-like anti-communist comrades of war-torn "divided nations," the Chinese Nationalists considered the ROK as the sole legitimate Korean government, to the extent that only the "Republic of Korea" or simply a unified Korea was shown on the maps published in Taiwan covering the Korean Peninsula during much of the Cold War era.

As a result, Taiwan virtually had no interaction with North Korea during the Cold War period; under the KMT's authoritarian rule, the DPRK was not only diplomatically unrecognized, it was a nonexistent communist state. In fact, the ROC itself was derecognized by the majority of UN member states and all intergovernmental organizations after it lost its China seat to the PRC in 1971 and eventually derecognized by the United States in 1979. Not until the late 1980s did scholars of Korean studies from Taiwan enter the DPRK. Following the end of the Cold War and Taiwan's democratization, the number of North Korea–bound Taiwanese tourists and businessmen increased as Taipei lifted its travel and commercial bans against communist countries and Pyongyang sought to earn hard currency by allowing more foreign tourists to visit the hermit kingdom. The loss of diplomatic ties with South Korea in August 1992 deepened Taiwan's already severe isolation in the international community;[11] at the same time, it represented a window of opportunity to develop economic and other relations with the previously invisible DPRK. In December of that year, high-ranking North Korean officials in charge of economic policy visited Taiwan in the name of promoting Korea's national industries.[12] Furthermore, in 1996, North Korea opened an office for tourism promotion and visa issuing in Taiwan. Unlike representative offices set up by other countries that officially do not recognize the ROC, this small office does not function as a de facto consulate or a sort of communication channel between the two sides. Occasional charter flights between Taipei and Pyongyang via mainland China airports have been operating since 1995. In 1997, Taiwan Power Company attempted to ship some of its low-level nuclear waste (i.e., no spent fuel rods) to North Korea for final storage at the cost of $260 million, but the plan to store the waste in an abandoned coalmine met strong protest from South Korea and gained international attention, citing safety and environmental concerns. Both Pyongyang and Taipei refused to back down, insisting that North Korea was capable of handling the nuclear waste and the deal was a legal commercial matter. Taiwan nevertheless scrapped the plan two years later, reportedly under US pressure. North Korean authorities demanded $10.1 million from Taiwan Power Company in 2013 for violating the contract.[13]

According to Taiwan's Bureau of Foreign Trade, Ministry of Economic Affairs, the island republic's trade volume with North Korea in 2012 was $52.91 million ($26.9 billion with South Korea); $11.07 million of that accounted for by exports. In other words, Taiwan was in deficit in this bilateral trade relationship.[14] Being the North's sixth-largest trading partner (the fifth for the South) in 2012, Taiwan mainly exported organic chemical compounds and medical equipment to and imported coal and natural minerals from North Korea.[15] Despite expressed concerns from the American Institute in Taiwan (AIT, the de facto US embassy) and the South Korean representative, the Taiwan-Korea Economic and Trade Council was established in January 2009 to assist Taiwanese enterprises to explore business opportunities in North Korea; its sponsor, the semiofficial Taiwan External Trade Development Council, also carried out market research there in November 2012.[16] Indeed, North Korea might well be a potential niche market for some Taiwanese firms, as seen for instance in its growing number of smart-phone users (mainly higher-income Pyongyang residents). Curiously, Kim Jong Un himself appeared to be using a Taiwanese brand due to information security concerns over other foreign (including South Korean) phone makers.[17]

TAIWAN'S NORTH KOREA POLICY AND INTERNATIONAL SANCTION LOOPHOLES

Getting closer to the similarly isolated North might yield some commercial interests for certain Taiwanese enterprises, but it is doubtful as to whether Taiwan could generate meaningful strategic leverage for sustaining its "international living space" by exploiting the North Korea problem. To maintain the island's existence as an autonomous political entity outside the PRC's orbit, Taipei has adopted two different approaches in its post–Cold War foreign policy (to be precise, the actual practice has been a mixture of both, but the emphasis varies depending on how the political leadership conceives "China" and Taiwan's relations with that China). The current approach by the Ma Ying-jeou administration is not to openly challenge Beijing's "one China" principle in exchange for a peaceful cross-Strait relationship focusing on closer economic cooperation. The previous approach, under presidents

Lee Teng-hui and Chen Shui-bian, was to lean toward the United States (as well as its alliance with Japan), Taiwan's most important "officially unofficial" security partner since 1979, against an ascending China. Rather than extract more concessions from Beijing or support from Washington-Tokyo, playing the "North Korea card" would be a highly delicate maneuver and would run the risk of provoking the PRC and alienating the US-Japan alliance simultaneously.

This helps explain why Taipei's North Korea policy has been generally low-key, passive, and deferential to the preferences of the United States. As will be shown later, Taipei follows Washington's position over the North Korea nuclear issue and has been participating in US-led embargos against transfers of sensitive materials and technologies to North Korea since 2006. Aware of Pyongyang's special (if not always cordial) relationship with Beijing, Taiwan likewise has not attempted to establish official ties with North Korea even when it was engaging in "checkbook diplomacy" (i.e., to lure countries to switch diplomatic recognition from the PRC to the ROC) under the pro-independence Lee and Chen administrations.[18] Officially, Taipei has distanced itself from Pyongyang to the extent that it requires six months to process DPRK officials' Taiwan visa applications and the director of the National Security Bureau openly described North Korea as a "regional security threat" in the parliament after Pyongyang's 2013 nuclear test.[19] Against the backdrop of mounting US concerns, North Korea was designated as a "strategic high-tech commodity export restricted area" alongside Iran by the Ministry of Economic Affairs in 2006;[20] a "sensitive commodity list" was issued that covered 392 items, including various types of steel and precision machine tools. On the other hand, people-to-people exchanges are not subject to restriction, and North Korean officials in charge of tourism and commerce have been able to enter Taiwan in their private capacity. In October 2012, Formosa Television reported that Cho Sung Kyu, deputy head of North Korea's state tourism bureau, was in Taipei to discuss the operation of charter flights with a local travel agency. Pressed by legislators, both the foreign policy and national security establishments claimed that they had no knowledge of Cho's visit until they saw the news report, although the same official appeared to have come to Taiwan "more than 10 times" and was even interviewed by the same TV station in 2011.[21]

Given Taiwan's absence from international nonproliferation treaties and export control regimes (as it is not formally recognized as a state actor) and its important role in world trade and the production of dual-use, high-tech materials and technologies, it is necessary to ask to what extent Taiwan represents a loophole in international sanctions against North Korea's WMD programs. Since Taipei started tightening up its nonproliferation controls in 2006, some companies and individuals have been caught with prohibited sensitive items in their exports to North Korea. The Royal Team Corporation, for instance, was found to have carried out fourteen transactions to supply precision machinery workstation computers via China and Macao, useful for North Korea's missile and nuclear weapon programs.[22] To complicate the matter, Taiwan's geographic location makes it one of the world's busiest transit and transshipment hubs for commodities, which means that malevolent actors might attempt to use it as a transit point for WMD-sensitive transfers.

In 2006, Meisho Yoko, a Tokyo-based company, exported freeze-drying equipment (which could have biological warfare applications) to North Korea through a Taiwanese trading company without the required permission from Japan's trade minister.[23] In another case that stemmed from the manufacturer's apparent unfamiliarity with Japan's export-control requirements, Tokyo Vacuum exported its vacuum pumps to a Taiwanese customer in 2003. It turned out that the customer, Trans Merits Co., was not the end-user; during the 2007 inspection of Yongbyon nuclear complex by the International Atomic Energy Agency (IAEA), the pumps were reportedly used at North Korean facilities to remove impure substances from plutonium.[24] In 2008, the owner of Trans Merits Co. was convicted in Taiwan of illegally forging invoices and shipping restricted materials to North Korea, and, a year later, prohibited from doing business in and with the United States by the US Treasury Department, on the grounds that he had been supplying "goods with weapons production capabilities" to North Korea since the late 1990s. In his recent plea agreement with US prosecutors, the businessman admitted that he sought to bypass the 2009 ban and had managed to ship a precision machine to Taiwan using a phony name.[25]

Overall, these sporadic cases may be insufficient to confirm that Taiwan represents a serious loophole in international sanctions against North Korea (at least not in the past few years),[26] but it is clear that Pyongyang has not stopped attempting to exploit this weak link. Some structural weaknesses, both domestic and international, can be identified in Taiwan's anti-proliferation controls. Determined traders might export sensitive goods to a third country with looser restrictions and camouflage them as flotsam before re-exporting the equipment. To make matters worse, Taipei has no specialized agency for monitoring potential proliferation of WMD material and know-how, and the National Security Bureau's North Korea desk is "extremely understaffed" to handle the challenge.[27] As far as the international dimension of sanctions loopholes is concerned, three factors stand out: First, the unsettled Taiwan question has not only excluded the island from international treaties regulating WMDs but also prevented it from participating in existing multilateral export control regimes (MECRs), which serve as an important platform for members to exchange information on emerging proliferation-sensitive materials and technologies, suspicious actors, and export license denials.[28] Likewise, Taipei has little access to international bodies that could help it pursue proliferators and their agents; even Interpol's I-24/7 global police communication system, which provides real-time information on criminals and criminal activities, is not available to Taiwanese law enforcement agencies.[29] With Taiwan being an "outsider" of the international system, international sanctions against North Korea have thus carried little sense of urgency for Taiwan, despite its continued voluntary compliance with relevant international treaties and UN resolutions. Second, many Japanese-made commodities in the past found their way to North Korea, legally or otherwise, because of geographical proximity and the presence of a large ethnic Korean community in Japan having ties with the DPRK. The deterioration of the Japan–North Korea relationship since the mid-2000s and Tokyo's participation in international sanctions have deepened Pyongyang's need to "diversify" its sources of acquiring restricted materials and technologies. Finally, not unlike an earlier North Korea tactic of setting up a joint venture bank in China (Hwaryo Bank) that works as a cover for the Kim regime's overseas transactions, some Pyongyang-associated firms are said to have disguised themselves as mainland Chinese-invested enterprises when doing business with Taiwan.[30] The possibility of a cross-Strait free trade pact (also known as the Economic Cooperation Framework Agreement, concluded in 2010) being exploited to bypass UN sanctions cannot be ruled out.

CONCLUSION

The irony of history has made North Korea an unwitting bedfellow with Taiwan since 1950, and both remain hot potatoes in contemporary US-PRC relations. The extent to which Taiwan amounts to the weakest link in UN sanctions against North Korea's WMD programs may have been exaggerated, but there is a limit as to what Taipei's own voluntary anti-proliferation controls can achieve without external supports that are only available to sovereign states. The management of the North Korea problem is, once again, complicated by the unresolved Taiwan question. How realistic, then, is the speculation that the United States and China might "trade" their respective interests in the intertwined Taiwan and North Korea issues? To be specific, Washington's "Taiwan card" could be a halt to US arms sales to Taiwan in exchange for Beijing's greater pressure on Pyongyang. A few Chinese scholars have entertained this idea in the opening years of the twenty-first century because of the rise of pro-independence forces in Taiwan and the revelation of North Korea's nuclear facilities.[31] However, the PRC government has gained greater confidence over the prospect of the Taiwan issue (hence there is less need to seek Washington's cooperation) since the anti-independence KMT's return to power in 2008 and Taiwan's deepening economic dependence on the mainland following the signing of the cross-Strait free trade pact. After all, the very idea of "trading" with the United States amounts to a recognition that Washington has the final say on what is supposed to be a purely "domestic" issue.[32] As a result, even though the US government has already quietly withheld new major arms deals with Taiwan during Barack Obama's presidency,[33] Beijing sees little need to reciprocate. As has been illustrated in Chapter 7 of this volume, China's move to participate in UN sanctions against the DPRK in 2013 reflected the results of its North Korea policy debates and was independent of its considerations of the Taiwan question. Beijing's "North Korea card" could be backing a hostile Kim regime as a means to punish the United States for supporting Taiwan.[34] The speculation that the PRC might do so to harm the strategic interest of or to create trouble for the United States nevertheless overlooks the former's broader goal of maintaining stability on its peripheries for a stable international environment conducive to economic growth.[35] Given that its reduced support for Taiwan has had no discernible effect in inducing more cooperation over North Korea from Beijing, Washington's current approach of sidelining security ties with Taipei seems misguided. In short, although the course of the North Korea issue and of the Taiwan issue has been intertwined, the policy utility of the aforementioned "Taiwan card" and the "North Korea card" may be more imagined than real.

NOTES

1. The author would like to thank Nina C. Krickel and Hung-lin Yeh for their professional research assistance.

2. Kenneth Waltz, *Theory of International Politics* (New York: McGraw-Hill, 1979), 72–73.

3. John J. Mearsheimer, *The Tragedy of Great Power Politics* (New York: W. W. Norton, 2001), 44.

4. Denny Roy, *Taiwan: A Political History* (Ithaca: Cornell University Press, 2003), 111.

5. Bruce Cumings, *The Origins of the Korean War, vol. 2, The Roaring of the Cataract, 1947–1950* (Princeton: Princeton University Press, 1990), 524–43.

6. The General Assembly later adopted the Resolution 505 on 1 February 1952 to criticize the Soviet Union.

7. On how the United States sought to rein in its small but ambitious allies through bilateral security institutions, see Victor D. Cha, "Powerplay: Origins of the U.S. Alliance System in Asia," *International Security* 34 (2009/10): 158–96.

8. John W. Garver, *The Sino-American Alliance: Nationalist China and American Cold War Strategy in Asia* (Armonk: M. E. Sharpe, 1997), 291. From hindsight, Eisenhower seemed to overstate the case of giving Chiang a free hand.

9. Roy, *Taiwan*, 125.

10. Having initiated two Taiwan Strait crises in 1954–1955 and 1958, Mao was told by Khrushchev in a meeting that China should accept Taiwan's independence. Garver, *Sino-American Alliance*, 141–42.

11. Although the ROK was the last East Asian country to ditch Taiwan in favor of diplomatic and commercial ties with the PRC (which dropped its objection against South Korean UN membership application in 1991), images of brotherly South Korea in Taiwan significantly darkened afterward due to the perceived "ungraceful" betrayal by Seoul (the ROK government confiscated the property of the ROC embassy, handed it to the PRC, and expelled Taiwanese diplomats in twenty-four hours) and, more recently, "unfair" competitions between South Korea and Taiwan in international trade and sports.

12. Lin Chiou-shan, *Qianjin Chaoxian—yu Beihan jiaoliu ershi nian* [Advancing toward Korea: Twenty-Years Exchanges with North Korea], second edition (Taipei: Sanmin, 2012). According to an unconfirmed Hong Kong news report, the delegation was involved in secret talks to establish diplomatic relations with Taiwan, but it seems more likely that Pyongyang approached Taipei to express its displeasure over Beijing's recognition of Seoul ("Taibei Pingrang mitan jianjiao ca jian erguo" [Taipei, Pyongyang Missed Secret Talks on Recognition], *Yazhou Zhoukan*, 22 December 2011).

13. "Yunsong he feiliao poju Beihan xiang Taidian qiuchang 3 yi yuan" [Plan to Transport Nuclear Waste Failed, North Korea Demanded 300 Million Yuan from Taipower], *NOWnews*, 4 March 2013, accessed 22 October 2014, http://www.nownews.com/n/2013/03/04/314321.

14. "North Korea Country Facts," Bureau of Foreign Trade, accessed 21 October 2014, http://www.trade.gov.tw/World/ListArea.aspx?code=7020&nodeID=977&areaID=4&country=b645YyX6Z-T&pw=3.

15. Ibid.

16. Ibid.

17. "Cong Beihan lingdao ren bu ai Sanxing Pingguo zhi yong HTC shouji kan teshu shichang maoyi" [North Korean Leader Uses HTC Phone Instead of Samsung or Apple: On Special Market Trade], *TechNews*, 4 February 2013, accessed 21 October 2014, http://technews.tw/2013/02/04/north-korea-htc.

18. The only known exception occurred in 1992 (see note 12). Since cross-Strait relations were in a honeymoon period right after the end of the Cold War, it seems more plausible that Taipei mainly used its secret talks with Pyongyang to punish Seoul for its "betrayal."

19. Yang Chih-chiang, "Tai shangpin gongzhan Beihan li wei: Bawo shangji" [North Korean Market Captured by Taiwanese Goods, Business Opportunities Seized: Legislator], *Taiwan Xingbao*, 15 April 2013.

20. "Sensitive Commodity List for North Korea and Iran," Bureau of Foreign Trade, accessed 26 October 2014, http://www.trade.gov.tw/Pages/Detail .aspx?nodeID=901&pid=349342&dl_DateRange=all&txt_SD=&txt_ED =&txt_Keyword=&Pageid=0. Citing WikiLeaks, *Apple Daily* reported on 9 November 2011 that Taiwan's deputy defense minister admitted to the AIT in 2006 that Taipei "in the past" had exported small arms and other defense items to "objectionable" states such as Iran and North Korea.

21. "Beihan gaoguan mi fang Tai yezhe: Zhishao laile 10 ci" [North Korean High-ranking Official's Secret Visits to Taiwan, At Least 10 Times: Industry], *NOWnews*, 17 October 2012, accessed 26 October 2014, http:// www.nownews.com/n/2012/10/17/333326.

22. Hungfu Hsueh, "Two Indicted Over Illegal Exports to North Korea," *Taiwan News*, 28 December 2007.

23. "Illegal Export Linked to North Clinic, Bio-War Lab," *Japan Times*, 12 August 2006.

24. Masako Toki and Stephanie Lieggi, "Japan's Struggle to Limit Illegal Dual-Use Exports," *Bulletin of the Atomic Scientists*, 5 September 2008.

25. "US Charges Two Taiwanese over North Korea Ties," *Taipei Times*, 8 May 2013; Jason Meisner, "Taiwan Businessman Admits Violating Ban on Exporting Machinery," *Chicago Tribune*, 11 October 2014.

26. In addition to now tougher anti-proliferation measures, North Korean actions in Taiwan are constrained by the absence of DPRK diplomatic personnel (unlike in China) and the lack of ethnic Korean permanent residents sympathetic to Pyongyang's cause (unlike in Japan). The author cannot find data regarding the number of DPRK passport-holders residing in Taiwan from the National Immigration Agency's website, accessed 25 October 2014, http://www.immigration.gov.tw.

27. Personal communication with a knowledgeable Taiwanese North Korea expert in December 2013.

28. Togzhan Kassenova, "Global Non-Proliferation and the Taiwan Dilemma," *Global Asia*, 22 March 2012.

29. Ibid.

30. See note 27.

31. Wu Xinbo, *U.S. Security Policy in Asia: Implications for China-U.S. Relations*, Brookings Working Papers by CEAP Visiting Fellows (Washington, DC: Brookings Institution, September 2000), accessed 30 October 2014, http:// www.brookings.edu/research/papers/2000/09/northeastasia-xinbo; Yuan

Peng, *The Taiwan Issue in the Context of New Sino–U.S. Strategic Cooperation*, Brookings Working Papers by CEAP Visiting Fellows (Washington, DC: Brookings Institution, Summer 2004), 24, 25 and 29.

32. Chinese leaders have hinted at the possibility of "freezing" ballistic missiles targeting Taiwan for suspending US arms sales to the island, which, unlike accepting the "Taiwan card," would not create the same legitimizing effect for Washington. John Pomfret, "China Suggests Missile Buildup Linked to Arms Sales to Taiwan," *Washington Post*, 10 December 2002.

33. Note that the White House as of October 2014 has only approved items that the George W. Bush administration agreed to sell in April 2001 or are already in the Taiwan military's arsenal. Ching-Chang Chen, "When Is China's Military Modernization Dangerous? Constructing the Cross-Strait Offense-Defense Balance and U.S. Arms Sales to Taiwan," *Issues & Studies* 45, no. 3 (2009): 69–119.

34. Richard C. Bush, "Taiwan Comes Between the U.S. and China Again," *Los Angeles Times*, 11 February 2010; and Niu Xinchun, "Trust between China and the United States Beset by Problems and Challenges," *China–US Focus*, 14 February 2011, accessed 30 October 2014, http://www.chinausfocus.com /foreign-policy/strategic-mutual-trust-between-china-and-the-united-states -concepts-problems-and-challenges.

35. On the fear of entrapment, see Glenn H. Snyder, *Alliance Politics* (Ithaca: Cornell University Press, 2007).

CHAPTER 11

Common Interest Without Coordination

Utpal VYAS
Ching-Chang CHEN
Denny ROY

The previous chapters have detailed the profound negative consequences of Pyongyang's policies, including humanitarian disaster for the North Korean people, serious damage to efforts to slow the global proliferation of weapons of mass destruction, and increased tensions and a persistent risk of war on the Korean Peninsula. The domestic political predicament of the North Korean regime drives it toward hostile rather than cooperative relations with the ROK, the United States, and Japan. It is difficult to foresee that under the Kim regime the interests of North Korean elites could realign to an extent that they would see denuclearization, rapprochement with Seoul, and economic liberalization as their best options. Yet this is the challenge facing the region: to induce, if possible through non-violent means, Pyongyang to choose a policy path wished for by all the other Northeast Asian governments.

None of the authors in this volume is optimistic about the likelihood of close regional coordination bringing about either denuclearization or a dramatic improvement in the human rights situation in North Korea. They offer at least seven concrete approaches to dealing with the DPRK crisis. Unfortunately, each of these approaches has serious limitations.

1. *Deny the technology and materials North Korea needs for nuclear weapons and missile development*

Unfortunately, international efforts have already failed to stop the DPRK from building working nuclear explosives. North Korea's pursuit of a uranium-based weapon in addition to a plutonium-fueled bomb further reduces the outside world's capability to stymie DPRK development work. North Korea contains abundant recoverable uranium deposits. DPRK technicians are apparently making progress toward robust long-range missiles and warhead miniaturization in spite of international nonproliferation protocols.

2. *Work to subvert the regime by undermining its public support*

By all accounts, many North Koreans now see glimpses of media from the outside world despite the best efforts of their government to retain totalitarian control over information. Continuing to smuggle in leaflets and DVDs that exposes the regime's failings could in theory help inspire a popular revolt that would topple the regime and possibly open the door to a new government that would seek peace, economic openness, and better treatment of the North Korean people. There are, however, two large problems with this prospective solution. First, the increasing awareness of the North Korean people that their country is relatively poor does not necessarily turn them against their own government because many accept the government's continually repeated argument that the DPRK's economic difficulties are the result of hostility on the part of a superpower that seeks to destroy North Korea. Second, even if they wanted to rebel, ordinary North Koreans lack the means to organize and to arm themselves.

3. *Persuade China to stop propping up the regime*

China is certainly the external power with the greatest influence over North Korea—a major supplier of basic necessities such as food and energy, the DPRK's main trading partner, and Pyongyang's protector in the UN Security Council. A Chinese decision to work for the overthrow of the Kim regime might have pivotal results. It is clear, however, that China prefers the status quo of nuclear-armed North Korean brinksmanship under the command of the crass and callow Kim Jong Un to the dangers that would stem from regime collapse. While the Chinese understate the extent of their influence over the DPRK as a negotiating tactic with Americans, Beijing is more sensitive than the United States to the limits of China's ability to make North Korea's leaders act against their own perceived interests. Although many Chinese commentators have reached the conclusion that Pyongyang's behavior does not support China's interests, this sentiment would have to reach much higher levels for China to support a change of government. Chinese frustration is therefore manageable for Pyongyang.

4. *Increase foreign economic cooperation with North Korea to strengthen the DPRK's disincentives for outlaw behavior*

To the extent that Pyongyang sees foreign trade and investment as valuable, presumably the DPRK government will try harder to avoid actions that might endanger the inflow of economic benefits. Greatly increased trade and investment, then, might succeed where sanctions and military deterrence failed in moderating DPRK behavior. Since Pyongyang has taken denuclearization off the table, this approach would amount to trade first with the hope that reduced tensions and ultimately denuclearization would follow. But for Washington, Seoul, and Tokyo, the lifting of sanctions against Pyongyang without denuclearization or a comparably substantial concession by North Korea is politically close to impossible and would open each of these governments to severe domestic criticism. Although China pursues a robust economic relationship with the DPRK, this has not prevented the DPRK government from regularly defying Chinese wishes.

5. *Offer North Korea a US-DPRK peace treaty and nonaggression pledge from Seoul and Washington in exchange for DPRK denuclearization*

This approach is questionable on three grounds. First, recent DPRK policy evinces an interest not in bargaining away the nuclear weapons program, but rather in getting Washington to accept North Korea as a nuclear weapons state. Indeed, as we have seen, the regime extolls nuclear weapons as a major achievement and legacy of the otherwise grim Kim Jong Il era. Second, Washington and Seoul have previously offered numerous official statements of non-intent to invade North Korea—statements that are highly credible since the two governments have demonstrated aversion to that option even in the face of persistent DPRK belligerence. Additional assurances may not bring about a change in the DPRK's posture because it is not clear that the regime wants to reduce tensions. Maintaining a permanent war footing bolsters the regime's domestic legitimacy by supplying an excuse for the country's lack of prosperity and a source for claims that the leadership is successfully protecting the country from hostile foreign powers. Third, the DPRK's record of breaking or cheating on international agreements raises the suspicion that even if Pyongyang was to seemingly reverse course and agree to trade its nuclear weapons program for economic and political rewards, there is a high likelihood that the agreement would break down soon after North Korea pocketed the concessions offered by its adversaries.

6. *Build confidence in inter-Korea relations by promoting relatively easy forms of cooperation, such as tourism and family reunions*

This approach fits the assumption that a benign ROK will make the North Korea government feel more secure, leading to a melting away of DPRK hostility. Confidence-building makes sense if Pyongyang is mistakenly worried about a nonexistent ROK intention to invade the North. In that case nonsensitive joint activities could help allay North Korea's fears. If, however, Pyongyang is worried about peaceful absorption by South Korea or by the loss of an external enemy on which to blame the DPRK government's failures, the presumption that Pyongyang is interested in confidence-building is questionable.

7. *Initiate Five-Party Talks, without North Korea, to signal to Pyongyang the region's willingness to cooperate and to formulate an approach without North Korean input*

This would be an addition to the many signals already sent to Pyongyang, to little apparent effect, that other governments in the region support denuclearization and most also condemn North Korea's massive failure to protect its citizens' human rights. While Five-Party Talks would reinforce a siege mentality in Pyongyang and might produce the temporary tactical response of an international outreach campaign by the DPRK featuring a few goodwill gestures, it is highly unlikely that the convening of the Five would alter the basic calculations within the Kim regime that have produced the nuclear and missile programs and the humanitarian disaster in North Korea. Furthermore, Beijing has shown itself highly averse to the perception that China is plotting with Pyongyang's adversaries behind the backs of the North Koreans, fearing this will weaken China's influence in Pyongyang. This reduces the possibility that China would agree to a multilateral meeting expressly called to discuss the DPRK problem if the North Koreans were not in attendance.

Unfortunately, it is hard to escape the conclusion that while other governments in the region can agree on their opposition to nuclearization and humanitarian disaster in North Korea, they cannot agree on a coordinated, effective strategy for solving these problems. Each of these outside governments has a unique assessment of the level and nature of the North Korea issue, and each would prefer to deal with this issue in a different way. Furthermore, even if the other major regional states including China agreed to support a coordinated approach, it is not clear that any nonmilitary method could persuade North Korea to give up its WMD programs or its human rights violations. The costs of this ongoing crisis are rising as the North Korean population continues to suffer and the DPRK advances toward a nuclear ICBM capability.

List of Contributors

Ching-Chang CHEN is an associate professor at Ritsumeikan Asia Pacific University (APU), Japan. He has been teaching various political science courses at APU, including field study programs in China, Korea, and Taiwan, since 2009. His current research focuses on critical security studies with reference to East Asia, non-Western international relations theory, and Sino-Japanese relations. He has appeared in media such as *Al Jazeera* and *NHK* and published articles in *Issues & Studies*, *Journal of Chinese Political Science*, *International Relations in the Asia-Pacific*, *Asian Perspective*, and *Perceptions*. He graduated from National Taiwan University and obtained his PhD in International Politics from Aberystwyth University, Wales.

Nicholas HAMISEVICZ is the director of Research and Academic Affairs at the Korea Economic Institute of America (KEI). He is responsible for political and security issues affecting the US–South Korea alliance, especially issues related to North Korea and inter-Korea relations. He is also tasked with leading KEI's outreach efforts to connect the policy and academic communities. Prior to joining KEI, Mr. Hamisevicz was the research associate in the Asian Studies Center at the Heritage Foundation. He was also a co-author for Heritage's publication of the *Key Asian Indicators: A Book of Charts*. Mr. Hamisevicz has an MA in International Communication from American University and an MA in International Studies from Korea University. He graduated with a BA in Communication Studies from West Virginia Wesleyan College.

Jihwan HWANG is an associate professor of international relations at the University of Seoul, Korea. Dr. Hwang also taught at Myongji University, and worked as a research fellow at the Institute for Peace and Unification Studies of Seoul National University. He holds several advisory positions in the Korean government, including in the President's Unification Preparation Commission, the Ministry of Foreign Affairs, and the Ministry of Unification. His research interests include international relations theory, security studies, North Korea, and Korean unification. His publications include "The Paradox of South Korea's Unification Diplomacy" (2014), "The Two Koreas after U.S. Unipolarity" (2013), and "Face-Saving, Reference Point, and North Korea's Strategic Assessments"(2009). Dr. Hwang graduated from Seoul National University and received his PhD in Political Science from University of Colorado, Boulder.

KASEDA Yoshinori is a professor of politics at the Ritsumeikan Asia Pacific University (APU) in Beppu, Japan. He received his PhD in Political Science from Northern Illinois University in 2005. His research areas include international security in Northeast Asia and Japanese foreign policy. He has published articles in such journals as *International Journal of Korean Unification Studies*, *Pacific Focus*, and *Perceptions*. He contributed a chapter to such books as *North Korea's Foreign Policy under Kim Jong Il* (Ashgate, 2009), *Peace Regime Building on the Korean Peninsula and Northeast Asian Security Cooperation* (Ashgate, 2010), and *North Korea and Security Cooperation in Northeast Asia* (Ashgate, 2014).

Jina KIM is associate research fellow at the Korea Institute for Defense Analyses and holds a PhD in International Relations from the Fletcher School of Law and Diplomacy at Tufts University. Her research areas include US–North Korea relations, nuclear nonproliferation, and Northeast Asia security. She has taught seminars on humanitarian intervention at Yonsei University and nuclear proliferation and terrorism at Tufts University, and has worked for the Korean National Assembly, UNESCO, and BBC. Her recent publications include *The North Korean Nuclear Weapons Crisis: The Nuclear Taboo Revisited*, "UN Sanctions as an Instrument of Coercive Diplomacy against North Korea," and "An Analysis of Political Instability in the DPRK: Identity, Interest, and Leader-Elite Relations."

Shinichi OGAWA has been visiting professor at Ritsumeikan Asia Pacific University since April 2009. Before teaching at the university, he served the National Institute for Defense Studies, a research organ of Japan's Ministry of Defense, as director of the Research Department. His studies focus on US-Soviet/Russian strategic issues, nuclear arms control, and East Asian security affairs. His most recent English article is "Conventional Deterrence and Japan's Security," an Internet publication of the Nautilus Institute. In the past he participated in several study projects, including a task force titled "Nuclear Order in the 21st Century," organized by the Japan Institute of International Affairs. He received his bachelor's degree in Economics from the University of Kanazawa, Japan, and his PhD in political science from Yale University.

Denny ROY (PhD in Political Science, University of Chicago, 1991) has been a senior fellow at the East-West Center in Honolulu since 2007. He specializes in Northeast Asian international security issues. Previously he was a professor at the Asia-Pacific Center for Security Studies. He has also held research and teaching positions at the Naval Postgraduate School, the Strategic and Defence Studies Centre at Australian National University, the National University of Singapore, and Brigham Young University. His latest book is *Return of the Dragon: Rising China and Regional Security* (Columbia University Press, 2013).

Yoichiro SATO is a professor of international relations in the department of Asia Pacific Studies at Ritsumeikan Asia Pacific University. He previously taught at various institutions including the US Department of Defense's Asia-Pacific Center for Security Studies (APCSS) in Honolulu. His published books include *Norms, Interests, and Power in Japanese Foreign Policy* (coedited, Palgrave, 2008) and *The U.S.-Japan Alliance: Regional Multilateralism* (coedited, Palgrave, 2011). His comments on Japanese foreign policy and Asian maritime security have been published and quoted in various regional media including *Straits Times*, *Time Magazine*, and *Al Jazeera*.

Utpal VYAS is an associate professor (International Relations and Political Economy) at Ritsumeikan Asia Pacific University, Japan. He obtained his PhD at the University of Sheffield. He is the author of *Soft Power in*

Japan-China Relations: State, Sub-state and Non-state Relations (Routledge, 2013, paperback edition). His current main research interests are in China's financial and economic globalization, and regional politics in East Asia and Europe.

ZHENG Jiyong is an associate professor at the Institute of International Studies, Fudan University, China. He was a visiting professor in the IFES, Kyungnam University, ROK (December 2009–December 2010). Also he studied Juche Chulhak (Kim Il Sung/Kim Jung Il's Philosophy) at Kim Il Sung University, DPRK, as a visiting scholar (August–December 2014). His work on the domestic politics of the two Koreas and bilateral and multilateral relations related to the Korean peninsula has been published in the *Korean Journal of Defense Analysis*, among others. He is the author and co-author of over forty scholarly articles, and author or editor of five books, including *ROK's Political Party Systems* (2008), and *The 'Conflict-Reconciliation' Cycle on the Korean Peninsula: A Chinese Perspective* (2012).